STRONG
FEMALE
PROTAGONIST

BRENNAN LEE MULLIGAN · MOLLY OSTERTAG

Written by Brennan Lee Mulligan. Drawn by Molly Ostertag.

www.strongfemaleprotagonist.com

Printed in China

First edition

ISBN: 978-0-692-24618-4

Distributed in part by Top Shelf Productions

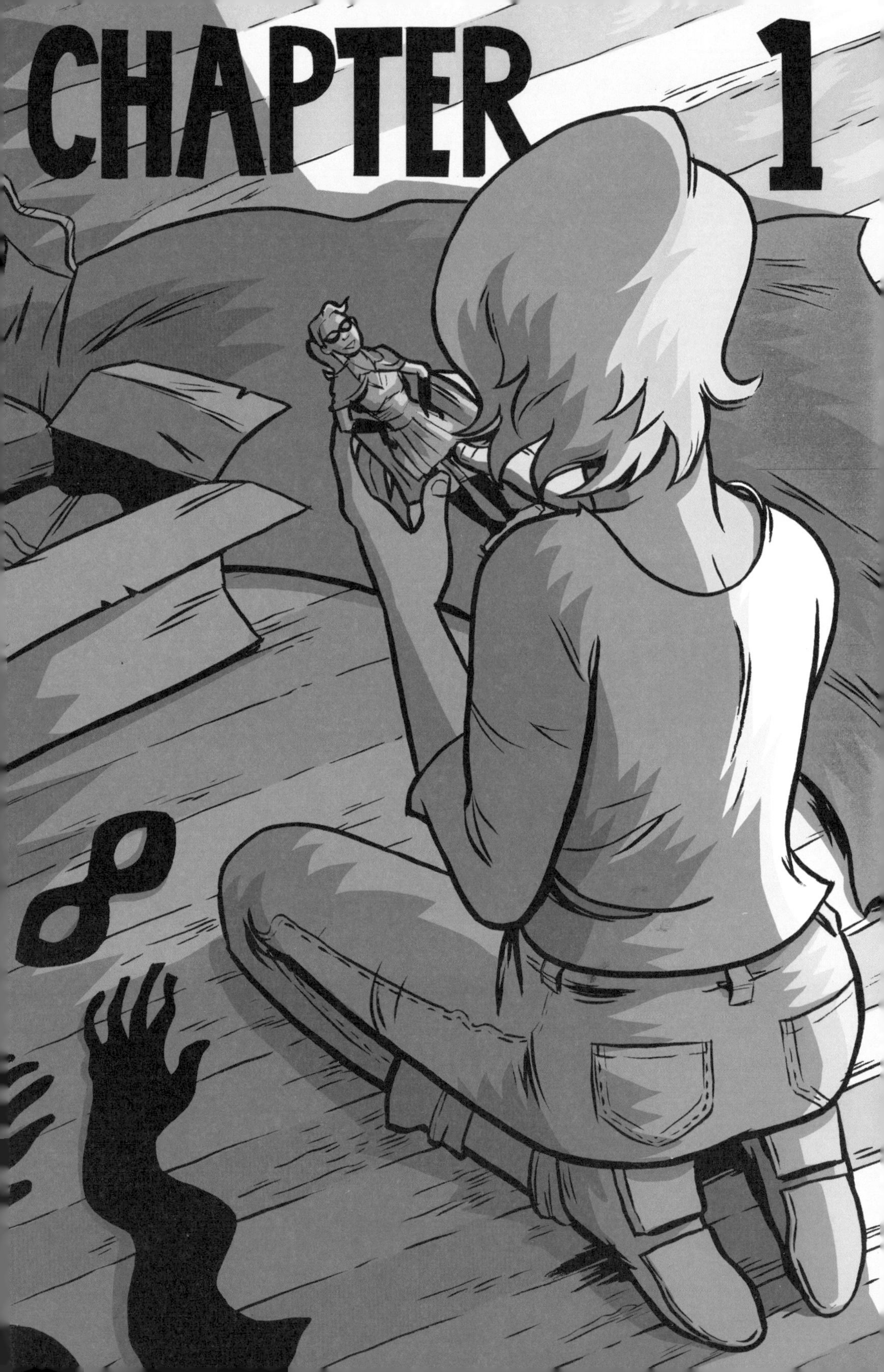
CHAPTER 1

The dog's name is Buster. He's a good boy.

To New York

Bronxville Train Station

Hey Dad, if you wanna head home, I'll be fine waiting by myself.

Nah, I'd feel better seeing you off.

That's a little silly.

I know. I just thought Christmas break would last a little longer is all.

Aw, dad.

Oop! There's the train!

Send me any papers you write, I love reading your work!

Okay! Bye, Dad!

Bye, Alison!

Bronxville Train Station

BZZZ BZZZ

From: Hector Jimenez

Hey Alison! Are you back in NYC yet? I'm flying in from Switzerland! Chance to catch up? Some pretty big stuff going on, maybe time to bust out that ~jumpsuit~ lol! let me know.

So sorry, PS, I'm going to a protest tomorrow and then I have to work at the firehouse.Maybe another time?

tic tic

In Alison's text message, the PS doesn't stand for post-script. WHAT COULD IT MEAN?

Rockin' those glove-mitten combos!

The expression in the last panel is how the creators of this comic look whenever someone yells "The tax payer, that's who!" in real life.

Do you mind?

Go ahead.

WE ARE THE 99%

Ugh, God...

Alison!

Hey, Violet!

Haha, how did I know I'd find you at the front of -

Hey, assholes!

Aw man, Alison ripped her cool new jacket! Thanks a lot, M15 bus.

Throwing fair-trade, organic coffee at the Man!

Let's be real. "I'm a fucking superhero" is not something a superhero should ever have to say.

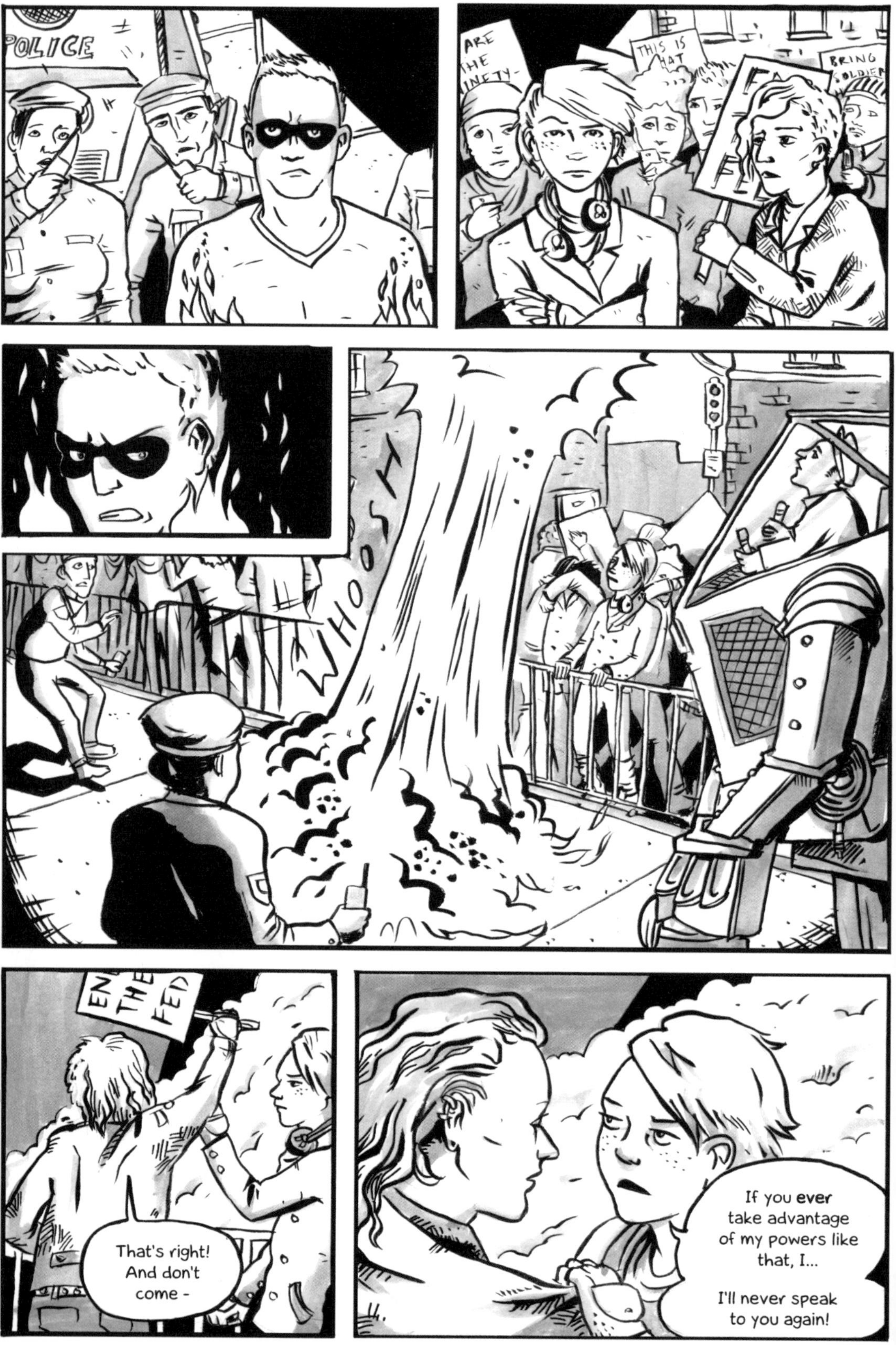
POLICE
That's right! And don't come -
If you **ever** take advantage of my powers like that, I...
I'll never speak to you again!

Alison isn't worried about a fight with Furnace, but she doesn't want her sweet headphones to get melted.

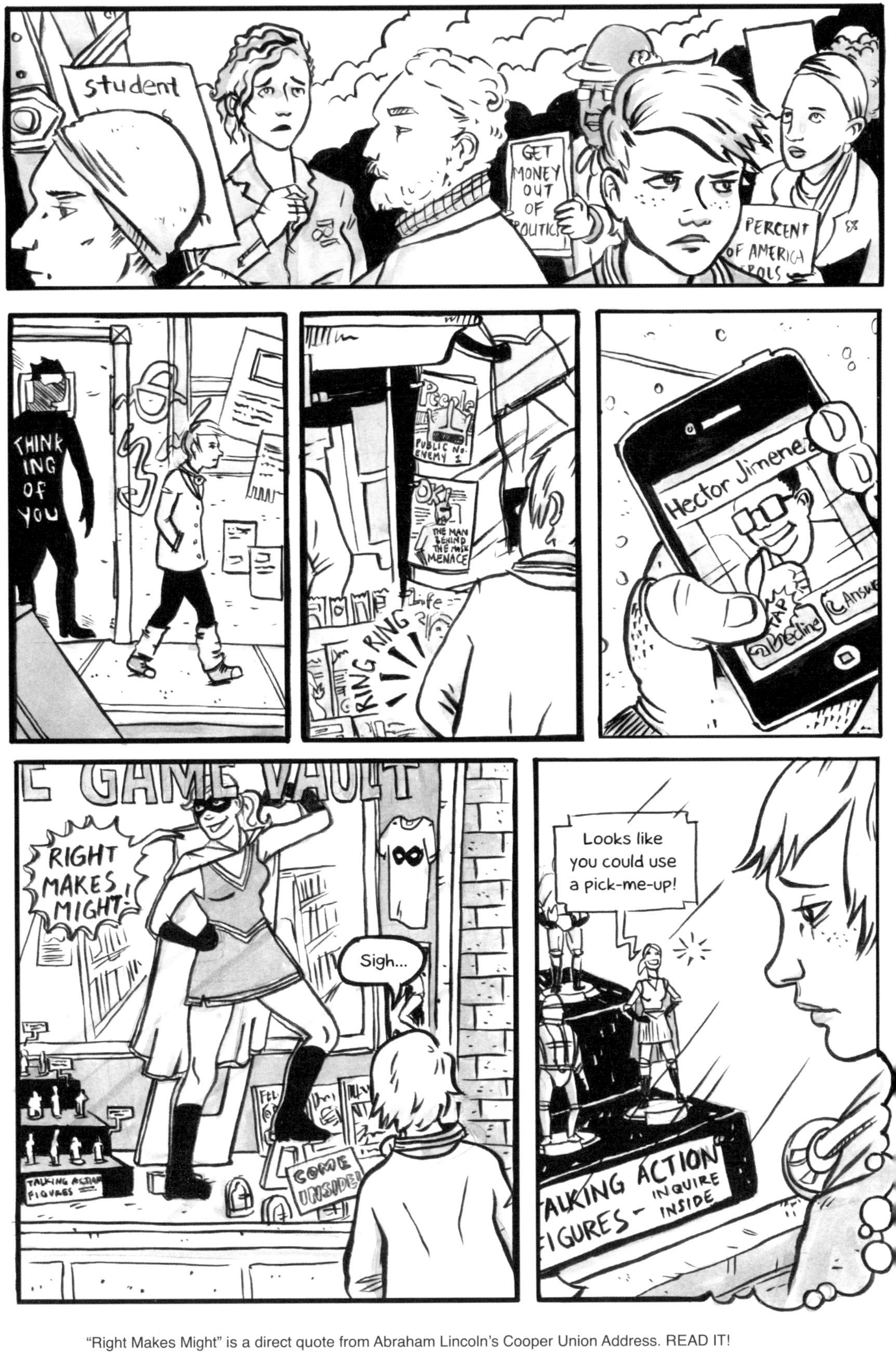
student
GET MONEY OUT OF POLITICS
PERCENT OF AMERICA
THINK ING OF YOU
People
PUBLIC NO. 1 ENEMY
OK!
THE MAN BEHIND THE MASK MENACE
Life
RING RING
Hector Jimene
TAP
Decline
Answ
GAME VAULT
RIGHT MAKES MIGHT!
TALKING ACTION FIGURES
COME INSIDE
Sigh...
Looks like you could use a pick-me-up!
TALKING ACTION
IGURES - INQUIRE INSIDE

"Right Makes Might" is a direct quote from Abraham Lincoln's Cooper Union Address. READ IT!

"System Error" is how robots say "God dammit".

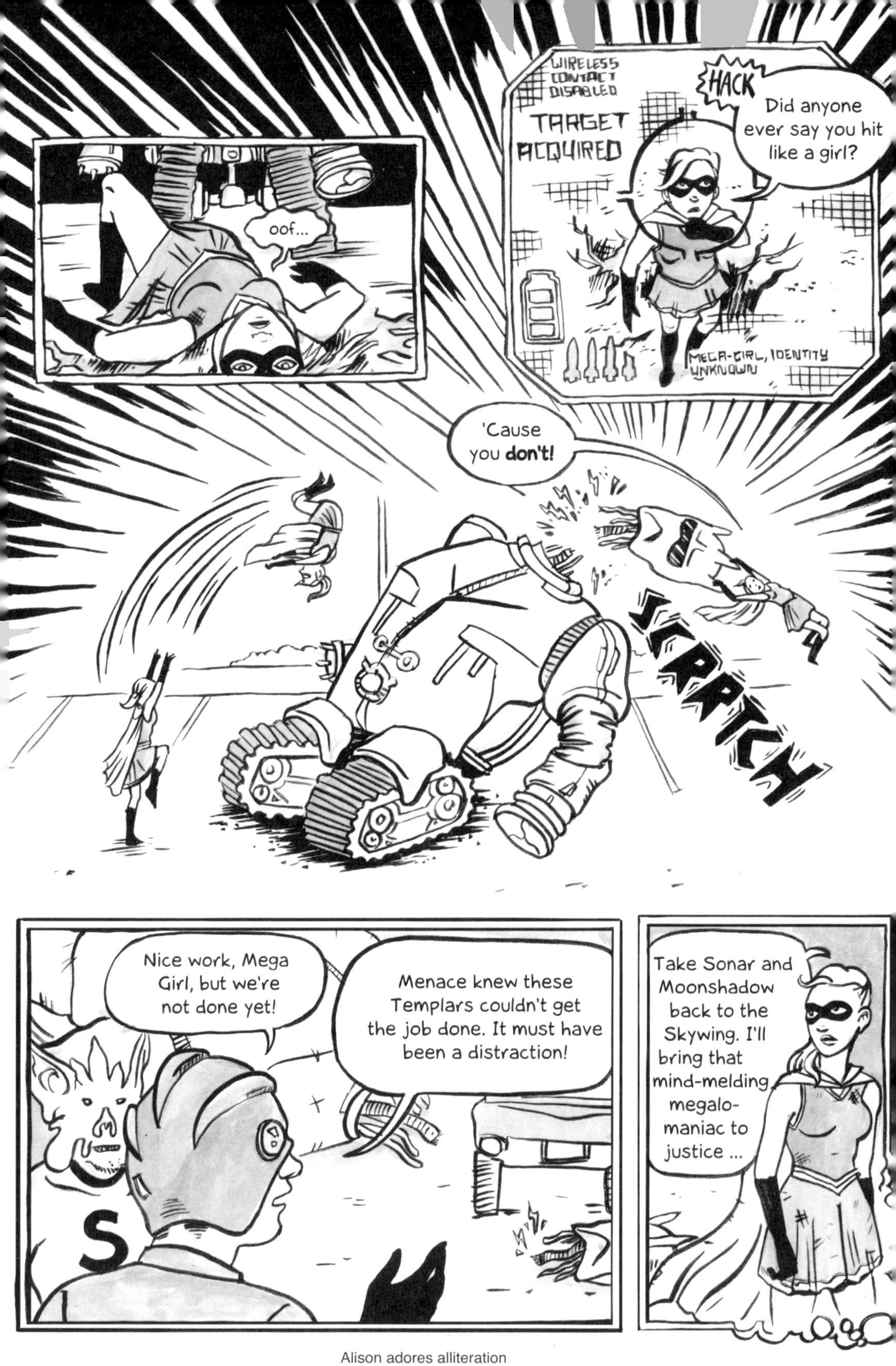
oof...
WIRELESS CONTACT DISABLED
TARGET ACQUIRED
HACK
Did anyone ever say you hit like a girl?
MEGA-GIRL, IDENTITY UNKNOWN
'Cause you **don't!**
SCRRTCH
Nice work, Mega Girl, but we're not done yet!
Menace knew these Templars couldn't get the job done. It must have been a distraction!
S
Take Sonar and Moonshadow back to the Skywing. I'll bring that mind-melding megalo-maniac to justice ...

Alison adores alliteration

...if it's the last thing I do!

THUNK

I got in a fight today.

Really?

I didn't see anything on the news...

Mom, I gotta go. I'll call you back.

CLICK

Hey.

Look, I didn't mean to scare you, I just...

Please! Don't. I'm so sorry.

I was really inconsiderate, I've just been so wrapped up in the movement...

Hey, it's cool, all's forgiven.

Friends?

Friends.

Those sweatpants look comfy as hell.

Being bulletproof sadly does not make you awkwardnessproof.

Dr. Rosenblum, this is embarrassing.

I think it's perfectly natural for you to be concerned about that. You're a very considerate young woman.

Thanks.

Now, now, no sarcasm please. If it makes you feel any better, I was much older than you when I met my husband, and he's the only man I've ever slept with.

What, too much?

A little.

I'm **sorry.** I thought being your federally-appointed therapist and doctor since you were fourteen might have bonded us **somewhat**, but if my friendship is **unwanted...**

I take it back, Doc. Tell me all the gory details.

Oh, please.

Alison, I wouldn't worry. I only bring it up because they're asking us to keep tabs on the reproductive habits of all you young superheroes.

But I will say this...

You are not 'super-strong', at least not biologically. Your somadynamism may be autonomic, but you certainly don't break your bed when you roll over in your sleep.

It is, on some level, under your control.

Frankly, you have more to fear from the fear of your power than your power itself.

"Autonomic Somadynamism is the scientific term for Alison's power.

I'm going to that concert tonight in the Village, you wanna come?

I don't think I can, I'm getting coffee with a friend.

Oh really? She's invited to come along, if she wants.

It's actually a guy, but he's only here for a few hours.

Oh, **I** see. You have a good time tonight!

It's not like that!

Hello?

Alison! Long time, no talk!

Hey, Pintsize!

Didn't you get my message?

Cleaver and Graveyard escaped, but Sonar thinks he's tracked them down to this bunker in –

Hector...

I know, I know, you're not a superhero anymore. But these guys are the real deal!

Cleaver's only gotten more powerful since you took him in. There'd be no cameras, I'll come pick you up in the jet, it'll take an hour tops, and we can get these guys back behind bars!

Hector...the military will probably be able to handle it, you don't need to...

The **military**?! Are you serious? You're **Mega Girl**!

...hello?

"Bluetooth headsets are cool, right?" - Pintsize

Hey, Hector?

Do me a favor.

Don't tell me who I am, okay?

Alison, I...

I'm not finished.

You're the only Guardian who still talks to me, so I'm sorry, but going on a mission with everyone sounds like something only **you** want to do.

Second, **I am not a superhero!**

GUARDIANS

JUNE 2012

Look, just shoot me straight. This isn't about Menace, is it? I know they used to work for him.

It's got nothing to do with that.

This is a secure line, you can say anything. If you're afraid of Menace showing up...

I'm not afraid of Menace.

Really?

Alison, he's the only villain who ever defeated you. **I'm** afraid of him, for Pete's sake!

He didn't 'defeat me'.

Well then how did he get away?

Hello?

THINKING OF YOU

Goodbye, Hector.

Imagine a world where the superhero summer blockbuster wins the Oscar for 'Best Documentary' the next year.

I've got you now, Menace!

BOOM

Ah, Ms. Green. I take it the front door was locked?

Can it!

The only locked doors you'll be seing are the ones in your cell block, because that's where you're headed!

Good. I surrender.

...what?

Is this some kind of trick?

No trick.

As you'll notice, all the Templar are powered down. Here, allow me.

My telepathy has a mind of its own, so I'm afraid I've already made your acquaintance. But my name is Patrick.

Why are you doing this?

You may want to read these.

Menace has got one of those really comfy mesh office chairs. So jealous.

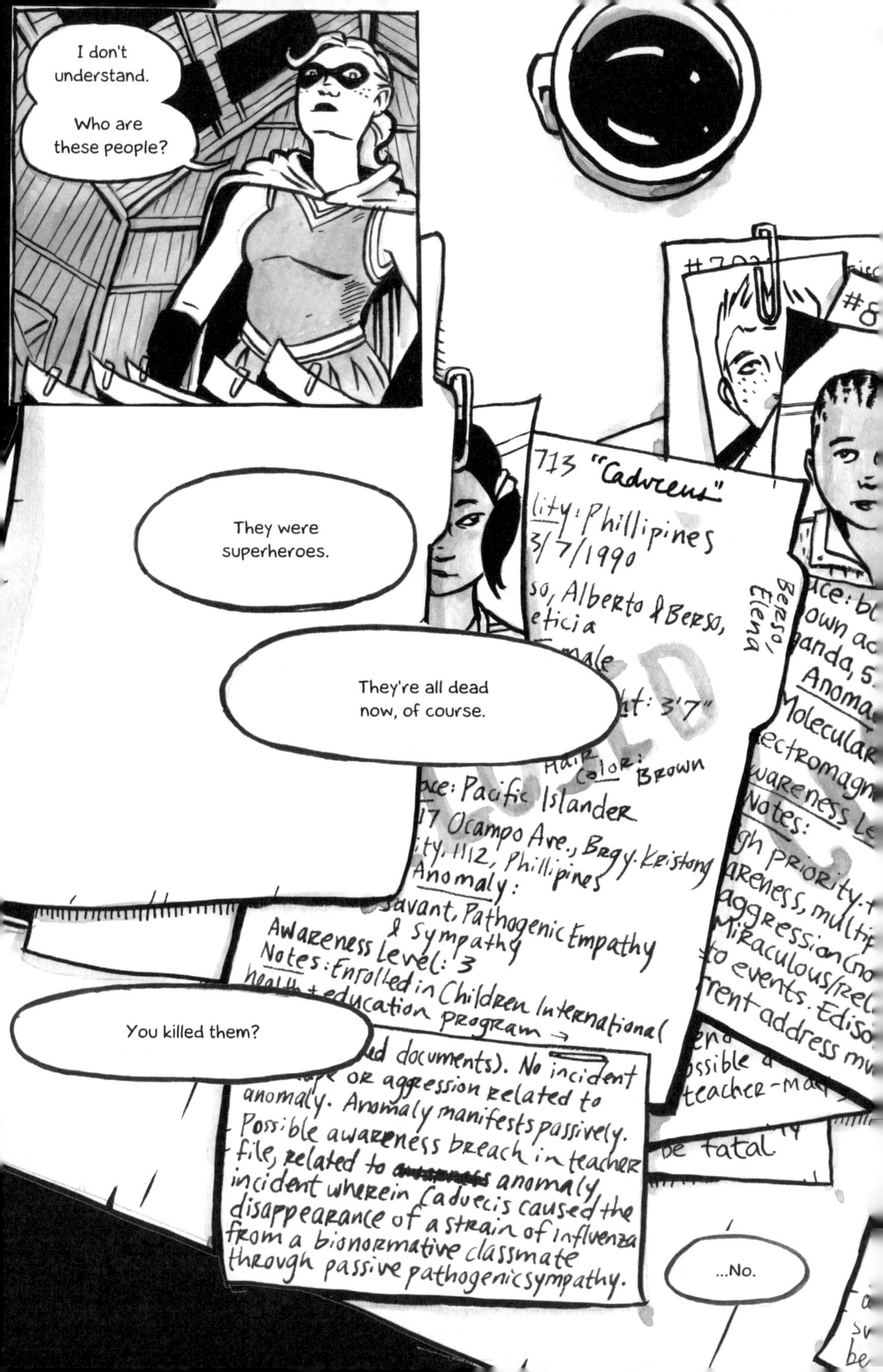
I don't understand.
Who are these people?
They were superheroes.
They're all dead now, of course.
You killed them?
...No.
713 "Cadvcens"
Anomaly:
Savant, Pathogenic Empathy & Sympathy
Awareness Level: 3
Notes: Enrolled in Children International health + education program →
documents). No incident or aggression related to anomaly. Anomaly manifests passively. Possible awareness breach in teacher file, related to anomaly, incident wherein Caducis caused the disappearance of a strain of influenza from a bionormative classmate through passive pathogenic sympathy.

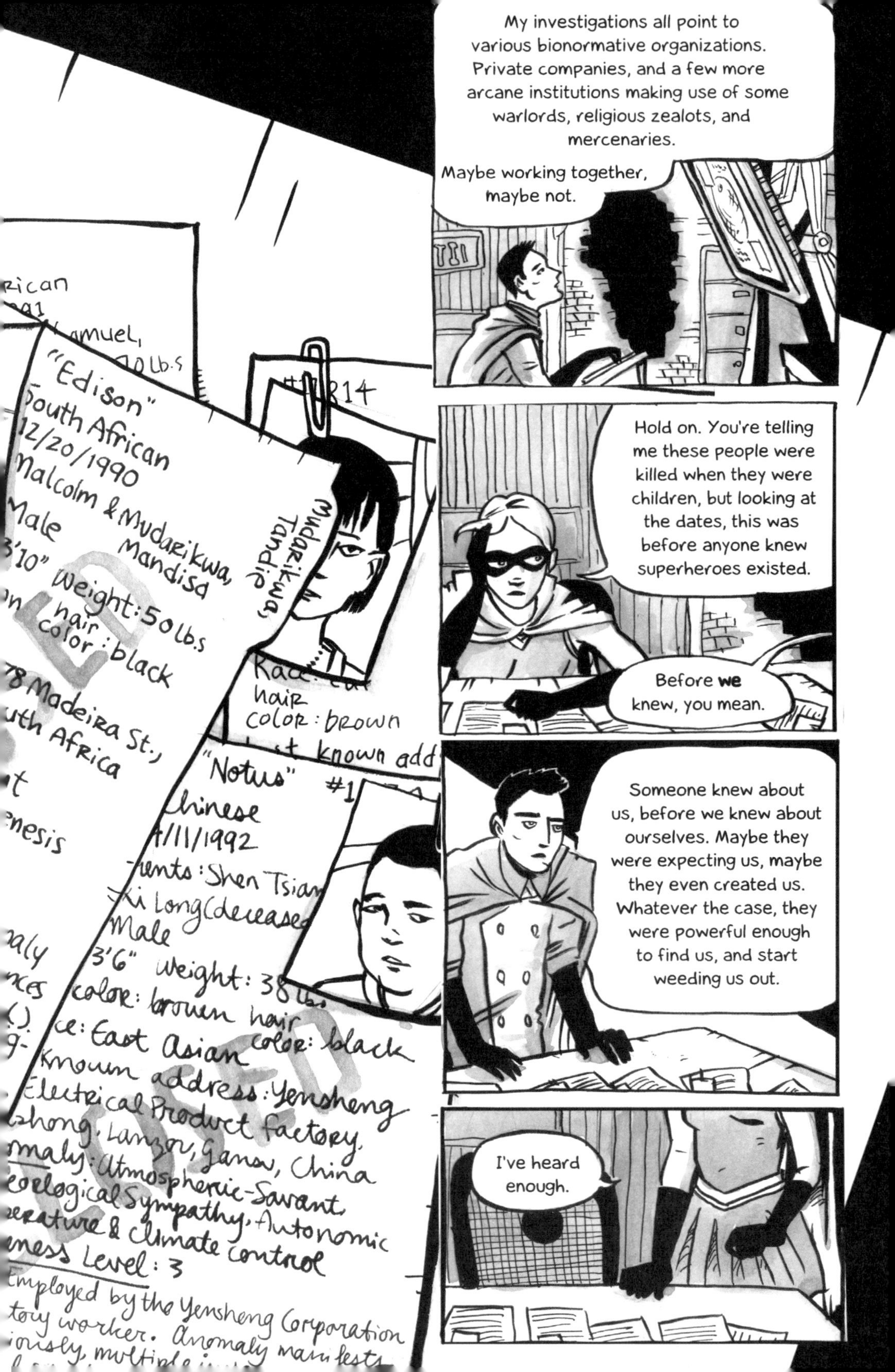
My investigations all point to various bionormative organizations. Private companies, and a few more arcane institutions making use of some warlords, religious zealots, and mercenaries.
Maybe working together, maybe not.
Hold on. You're telling me these people were killed when they were children, but looking at the dates, this was before anyone knew superheroes existed.
Before **we** knew, you mean.
Someone knew about us, before we knew about ourselves. Maybe they were expecting us, maybe they even created us. Whatever the case, they were powerful enough to find us, and start weeding us out.
I've heard enough.

I don't know what your deal is, or why you chose to reveal yourself, but it doesn't change that fact that you're a villain and a criminal.

You're going to jail.

HEH HEH

What is it? What are you...

You don't understand at all.

I understand plenty.

No, you don't.

Yes, I...

I'm reading your mind, and you don't!

A girl with the ability to communicate with diseases. A boy with the power to generate limitless energy. Dead.

Everyone who could have saved the world is dead!

The truth is this.

I'm not powerful enough to be a villain. And you're not smart enough to be a hero. Nobody's scared of us, or we'd have a little 'closed' folder of our own. What are you going to do, **Mega Girl?** Fling poverty into the sea? Smash all of us into a better tomorrow? Nobody thinks we can change the world, and they're right.

It's been lovely playing supervillain with you, Ms. Green, but it's time to put away the toys and grow up.

Mind readers must get really frustrated trying to explain things to people.

$4.17 for a pint of ice cream? In this economy?!

Engine 405, Hook & Ladder Co.

Superhero my ass, the kid's a god-damn liability.

You shoulda been here when we saw it on the news. John was going ballistic.

You're damn right I was! Furnace has caused more property damage and civilian injury than most supervillains. Where does he get off giving you a hard time?

Well shucks, guys! It's nice to know I've got you all looking out for me.

Of course, kid. You're a teenager, for Christ's sake!

Hey, I'm 20 now!

Really? I thought you were a freshman in college.

I am, but I took a year off to fight crime...

Hey, I gotta run, but I'll see you guys on Thursday!

Take it easy.

Alright, take care, Alison.

Alison.

She's family, for Pete's sake!

Patrick!

...the teacher is awesome, but the reading assignments are awful.

Sounds like a fascinating class. Makes me wish I had gone to college.

Yeah, how are you ever going to make something of yourself without a B.A., you poor, uneducated billionaire?

It's true! We had a board meeting at Templar Industries last week, and my CFO started quoting "The Miller's Tale." I felt so unprepared.

Happy belated birthday.

Aw, Patrick! Thank you so much!

WOMEN WHO CHANGED THE WORLD

RIGHT MAKES MIGHT!

How did you know?

Get a girl some chocolates, feed her for a day. Get a girl a book, and you haven't fed her at all. #donteatbooks.

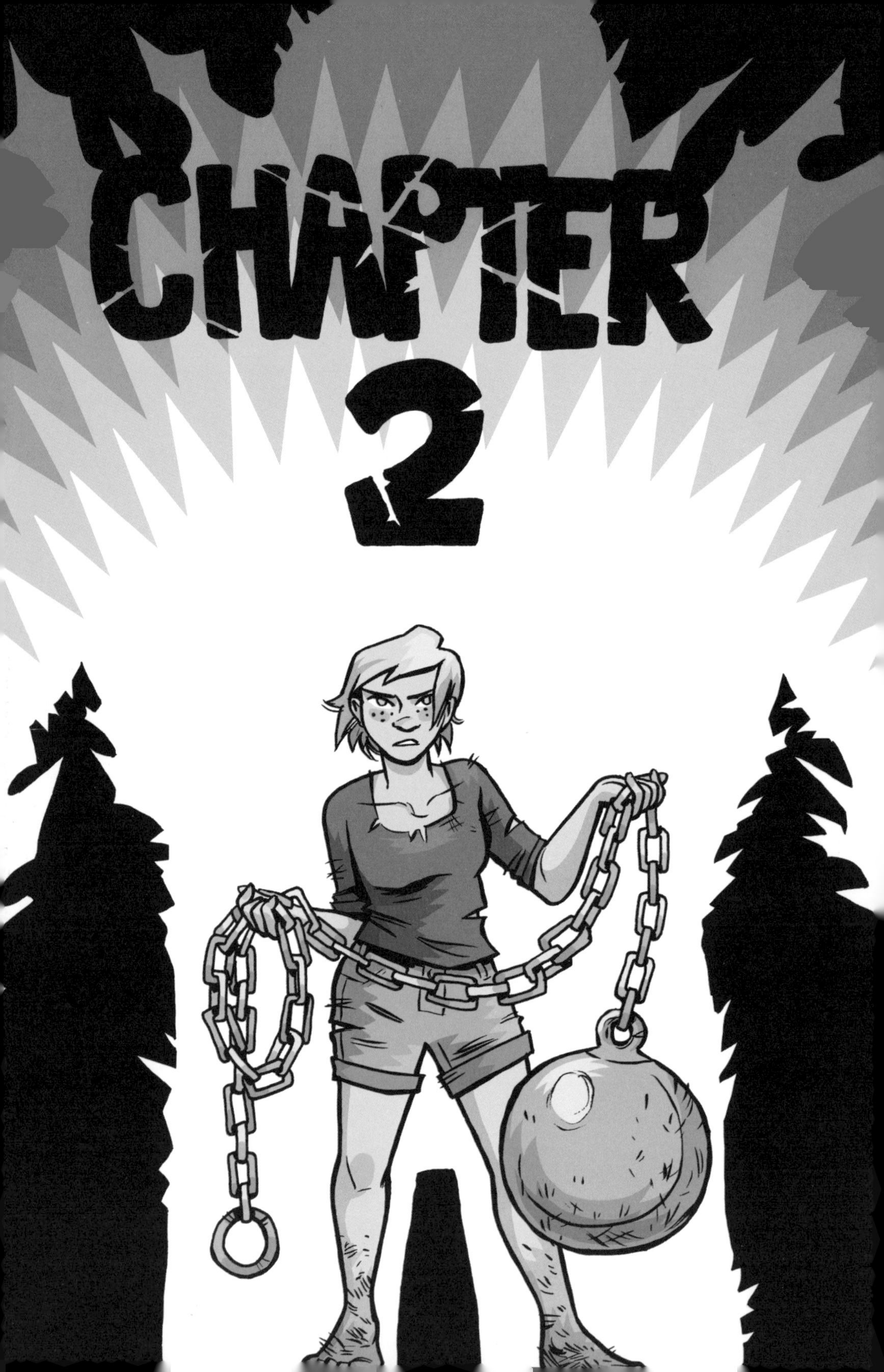
CHAPTER
2

Even superheroes have flying dreams.

Sleeping through your alarm is everybody's kryptonite.

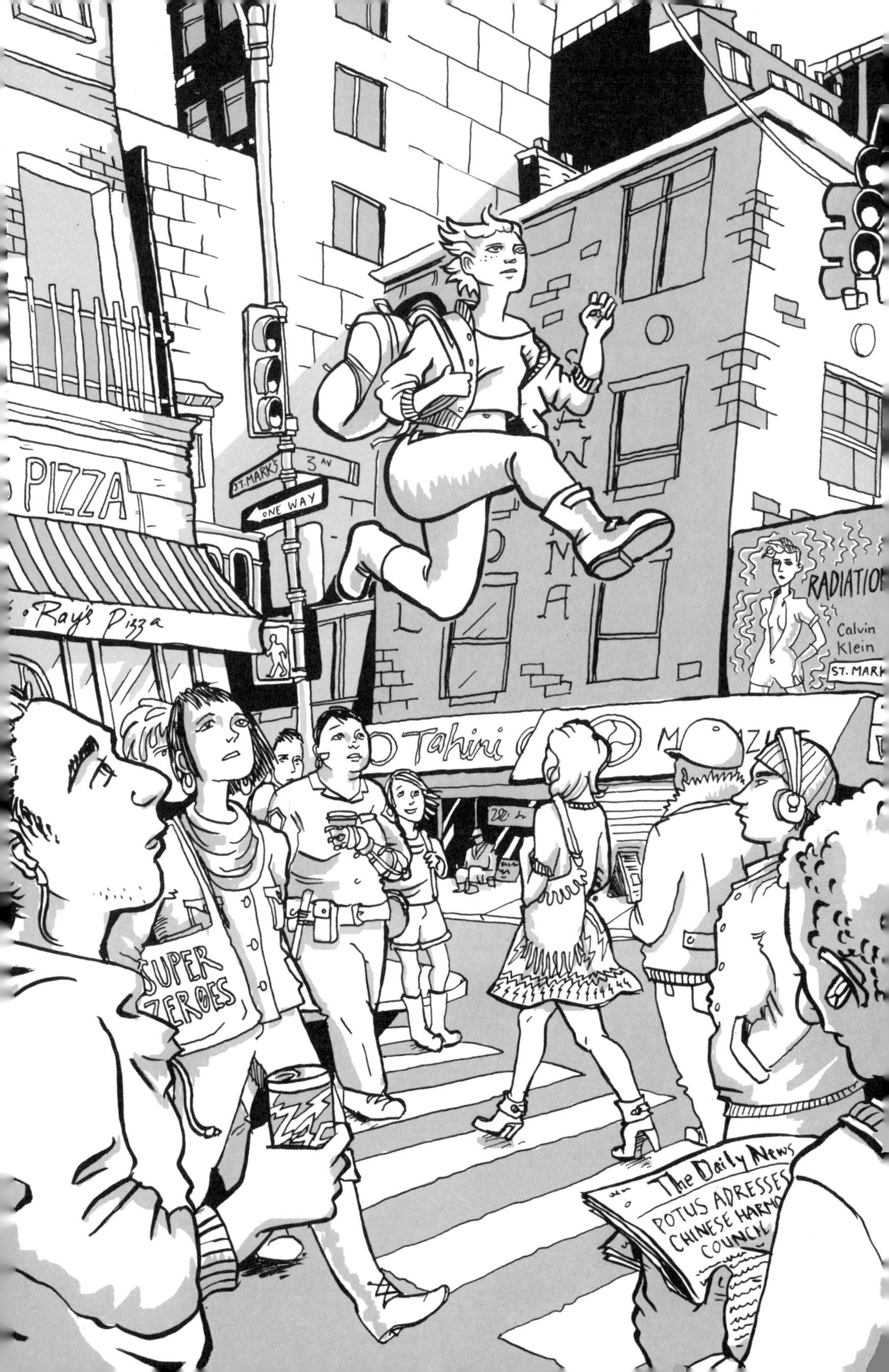
PIZZA
ST. MARK'S
3 AV
ONE WAY
Ray's Pizza
RADIATIO
Calvin Klein
ST. MAR
Tahiri
SUPER ZEROES
The Daily News
POTUS ADRESSES
CHINESE HARMO
COUNCIL

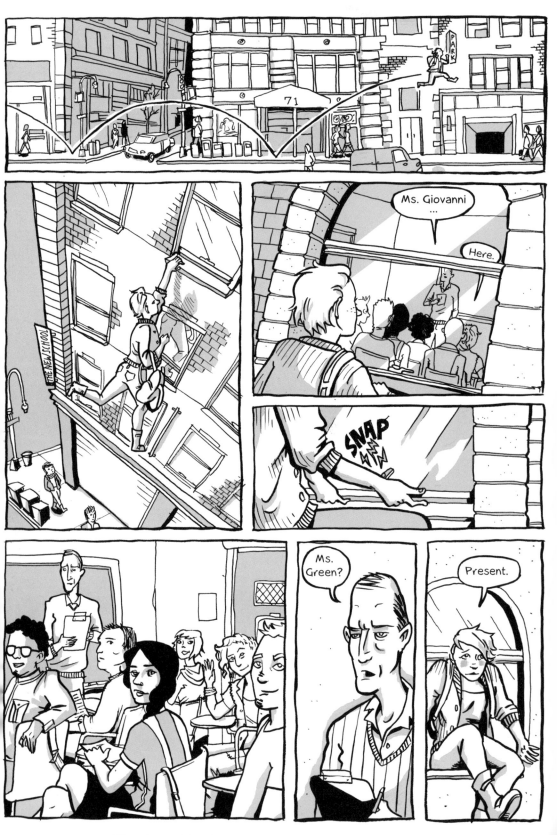

"If I can just sneak into the back of class, using my superpowers, naturally..."

Alison answered Question 2, which if you're wondering, was a way harder question.

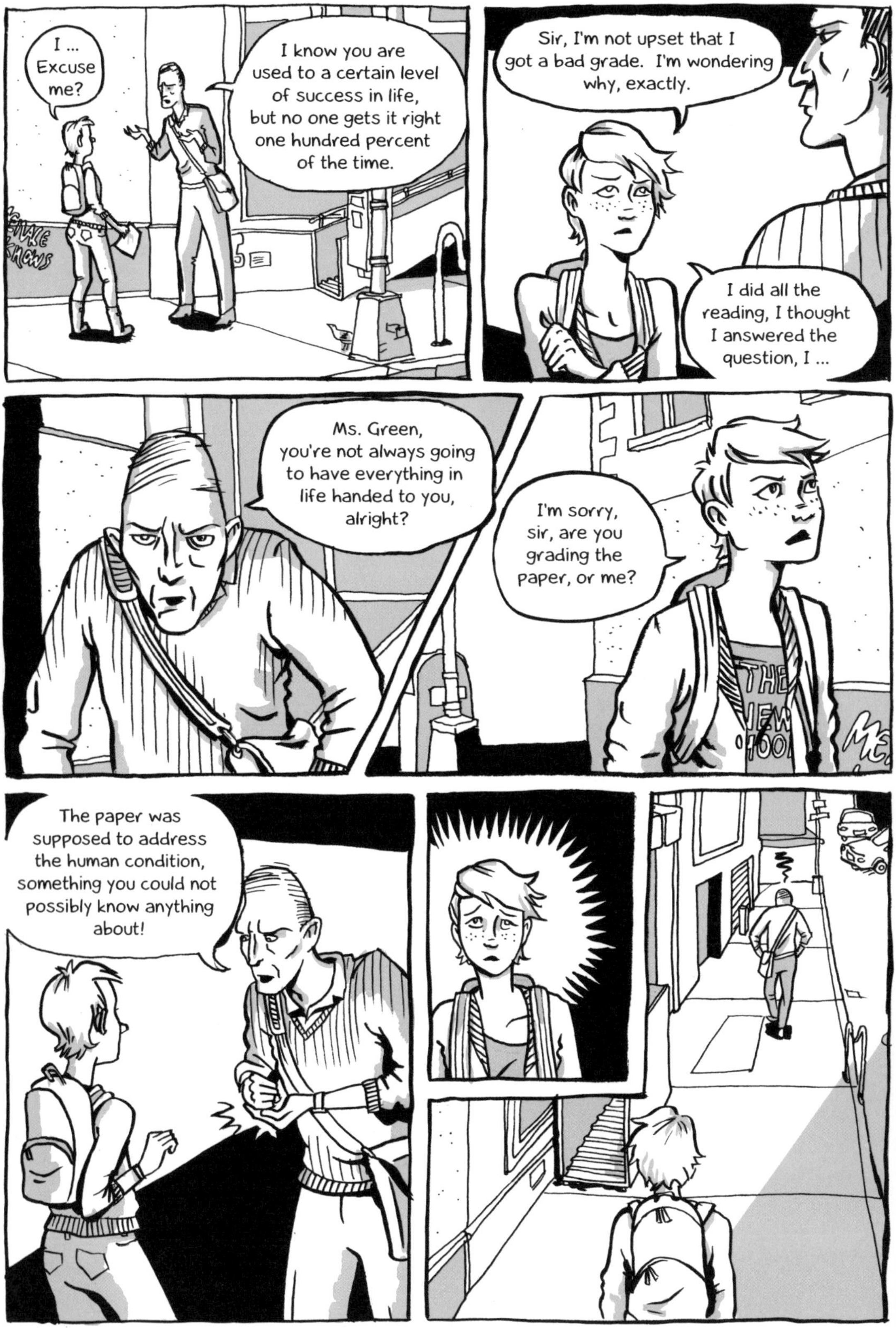
I ... Excuse me?
I know you are used to a certain level of success in life, but no one gets it right one hundred percent of the time.
Sir, I'm not upset that I got a bad grade. I'm wondering why, exactly.
I did all the reading, I thought I answered the question, I ...
Ms. Green, you're not always going to have everything in life handed to you, alright?
I'm sorry, sir, are you grading the paper, or me?
The paper was supposed to address the human condition, something you could not possibly know anything about!

Rude!

I just ... I don't know what to do.

It was so obviously a personal attack, you know?

Profesor Cohen has behaved similarly before, so I wouldn't take it too personally. I'm going to speak to the Chairman, and this issue will be resolved, I assure you.

Okay. I don't wanna get anyone in trouble, either!

It's fine if people don't like me, I just want to know if my paper was good or not!

...Rat?

YIPE!

Hey!

Wonder why they call him that...

Do you know how hard it is to find a nice spring jacket that looks good but isn't too hot?
Really hard, Rat, it's really god-damned hard.

One of the reasons that Alison's more reserved and awkward around regular folks is
that she's coming up with zingers NON-STOP.

Most superheroes would just have left the dumpster blocking the alleyway, but not Alison.

That landline phone at Rich's hacker-pad is blocked like whoa.

Rich! Don't drink that high-fructose soda, man! It's bad for you!

Like this guy, for example.

Look at the crack in that Dell's casing! Take better care of your stuff, Graveyard!

Well there's a lot of tier two and tier three super-humans with nefarious intent, and no crime is too small for the Guardians not to take notice...

Hnh!

... Mega-Girl, what course would you like to see the Guardians take?

... I don't know. Without supervillains, crime-fighting just seems kind of ... irrelevant.

You think you're above crimefighting?

Now that's...

That's not what I said! Look, I'm great at punching robots, but that doesn't make me any better at solving crimes. What is it exactly that I can do that the police can't?

What about the eventuality of a super-powered war with China? Would you feel obliged to...

Excuse me?!

Tandry Connors is not overly burdened by journalistic scruples, gang.

Don't just mention that casually in an interview! That would be horrible, and I hope that never, ever happens!

I think what Mega-Girl is trying to say is that while we would obviously fight to defend America, our first priority would be to stop a war from happening in the first place.

Oh, is that what I'm trying to say? Do you know how to stop a war, Pintsize? Cause I sure don't!

So you're saying you would not participate in a war between...

That's not what I'm saying!

Look! I've been in the Pentagon like four times, but I'm not really even sure what the Pentagon does! I'm supposed to fight crime, but I don't even know how laws get passed! I mean... Truth, Justice and the American Way? I stopped taking social studies when I was like fifteen!

I grew up in Westchester, and have never traveled anywhere else without this stupid domino mask on my face! Am I the only one who's scared that people are looking to me for answers because I can lift a car over my head?! This is crazy!

... Did... Did you just reveal that you grew up in Westchester, New York?

Alison is quoting 'Truth, Justice, and the American Way' because Pintsize made her read all his Superman comics when they were first discovering their powers.

That domino mask is now in Pintsize's office at the Guardians HQ.

That interview took place a little over a year ago. Cleaver and Graveyard were captured and imprisoned by Mega Girl over three years ago.

Alison!

C'mon, let's go dance! Now now now!

Whoop! Okay!

I'm not to not to love until it's cheap

Been there done that I've messed around, I'm having fun don't put me down, I'll never let you sweep me off my feet

THIS TIME BABY I'LL BEeeEEeeEE...

woo

cool!

BULLETTT-PROOF!

Did you ask the DJ to put this song on?

The creators of this comic make a small cameo. The expression on the author's face in this loud, hot nightclub is the most unrealistic thing in this superhero webcomic.

Yeah! I thought you'd like it!

Can we go?

... No, I make sure to hide my drawings in my binder so he could not find them!

Haha! What about you, Alison?

St. Mark's

Oh for sure. There was a boy I went to kindergarten with named Dylan Matthews, and I asked him to marry me. He said he wanted to marry Jenny Clark instead, so I made him a frog out of construction paper and gave it to him but he threw it in the trash.

No! He is rotten! You deserve better.

In his defense, we were five.

Why'd you make a frog?

It was the only thing I knew how to...

Addiction NYC
Tattoo & Body Piercing

FRIDAY the 13th DEAL

Guys! We're getting tattoos!

Mmm, bubble tea! Alison doesn't drink alcohol for safety reasons.

Oh my God, do you want to?

Look, $13 for any tattoo in the book! C'mon, let's do it!

Alison, what do you think?

Uh, that sounds awesome. I wish I could, you guys should totally do it without me...

Come on, you only live once, let's do something crazy! They're all like the size of a quarter!

No, I mean, I can't. I literally can't get a tattoo.

Oh shit! I hadn't thought about that!

It's okay, you guys should go for it. I'm pretty beat, I think I'll turn in.

It was nice meeting you!

Goodbye, Alison!

No tattoos, piercings, fillings, or tonsillectomies for our girl Alison.

Molly confronted Brennan about his obsession with trash cans after this page was drawn.
Brennan did not have a good answer.

Worth pointing out that most kids Alison's age did not get superpowers.

Alison belongs to a firefighter's credit union, but she's been researching other CUs for the seminar she's running.

Professor Cohen, can we talk for a moment?

That won't be necessary.

Professor Cohen, I'm so sorry about all of this. I didn't know what else to do, you seemed so upset with me, I didn't know...

Ms. Green, I don't wish to speak with you. I'm leaving.

Professor, please stop packing, I'm going to talk to the Board.

I'm not going to let them do this to you...

ENOUGH!

That photo was taken in 1982, ten years before Alison was born.

Do you want to know why I gave you an "F", Ms. Green?

Because you were criticizing Nietszche when you yourself are a living, breathing Ubermensch! What possible abyss could you have gazed into? The reason you feel like there are no monsters in this world is because you are one!

I don't... I'm trying to be one of the good guys. I'm trying...

I beg your pardon, a "good guy," did you say? What, because you roughed up some other aberrations?

You're like any other idiot, thug, soldier or warrior before you. Your existence is justified by fighting people like yourself. Do you see the tautology here?

WITHOUT PEOPLE LIKE YOU, WE WOULDN'T NEED ANY PEOPLE LIKE YOU! We don't need ANY of it! We'd all be better off WITHOUT YOU!

Look, I agree with you, but that doesn't mean you should hate me...

Alison had a daydream at the beginning of the semester that Professor Cohen would invite her out for coffee so they could talk about philosophy. Probably not gonna happen now.

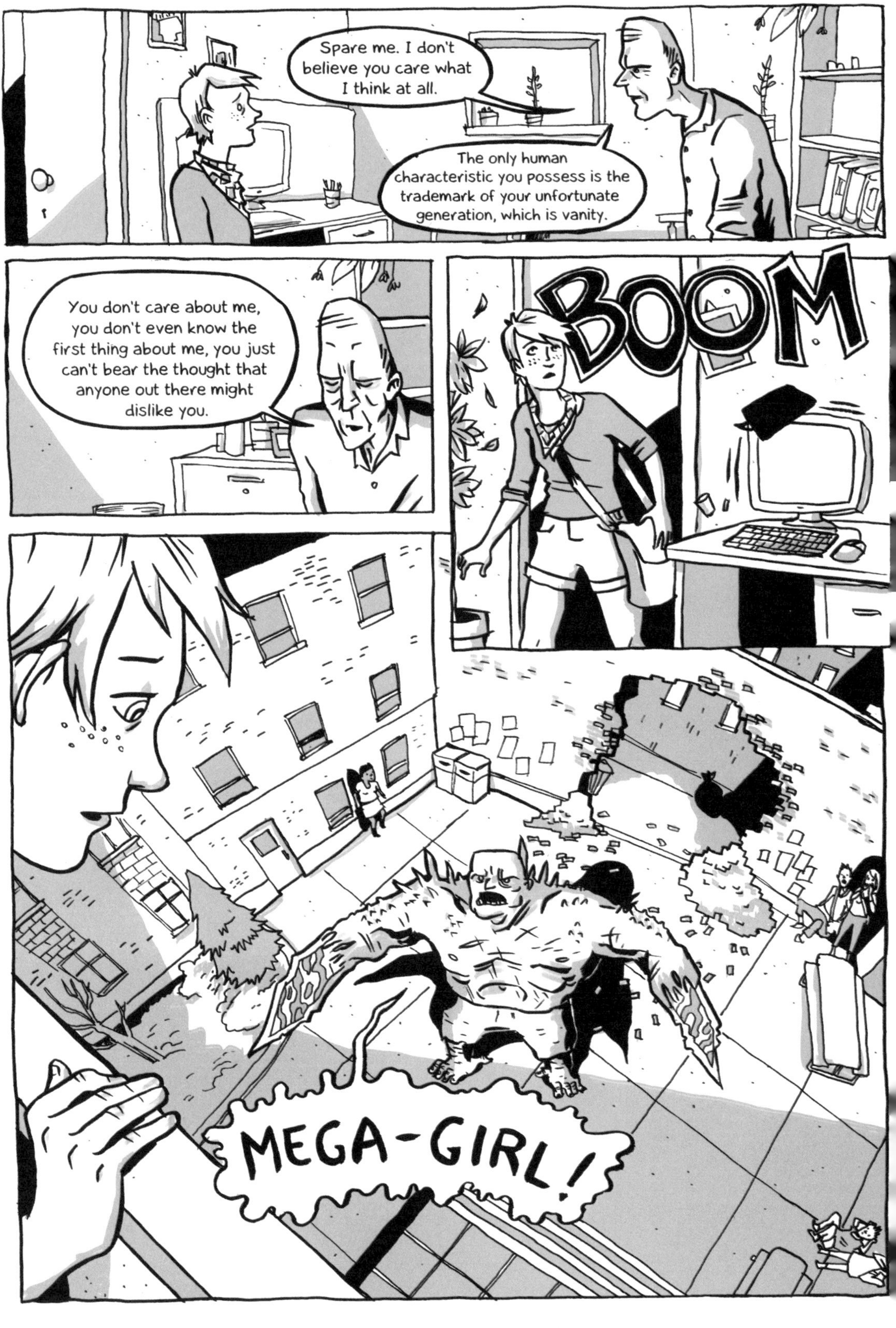
Spare me. I don't believe you care what I think at all.
The only human characteristic you possess is the trademark of your unfortunate generation, which is vanity.
You don't care about me, you don't even know the first thing about me, you just can't bear the thought that anyone out there might dislike you.
BOOM
MEGA-GIRL!

"Hold that thought..."

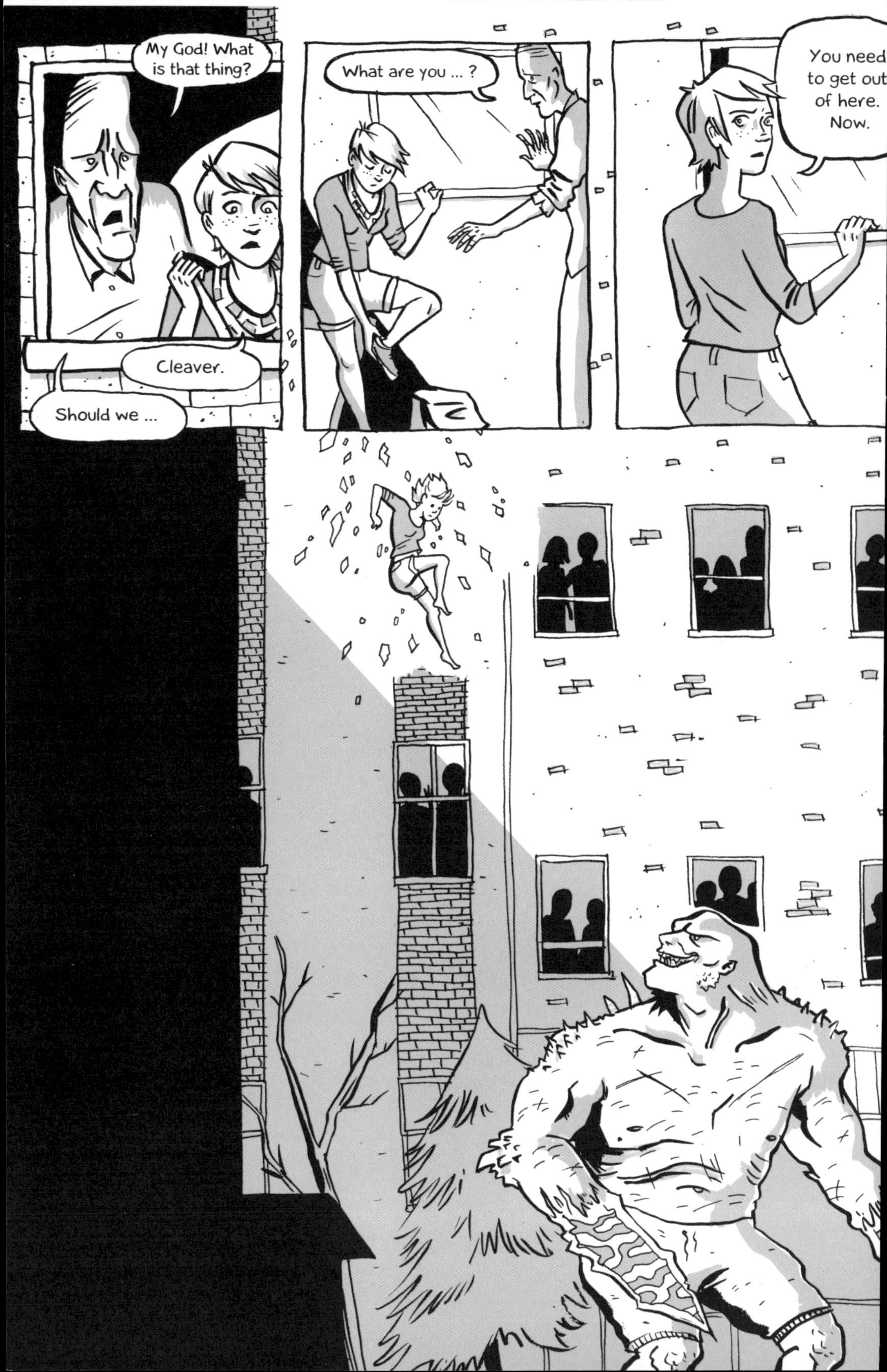

My God! What is that thing?
Cleaver.
Should we ...
What are you ... ?
You need to get out of here. Now.

What the...

Alison is in trouble!

Cleaver's at her school, he's calling her out!

And?

Are you kidding me!? We need to go help her! Brad, you're coming, right?

I mean, I don't think...

UNBELIEVABLE!

If anyone needs me, I'll be SAVING THE WORLD! BY MYSELF!

Don't worry, the Guardians have a whole bunch of high-tech reconaissance gear, but Twitter turns out to be pretty damn useful.

Good day to have neglected your homework, I suppose!

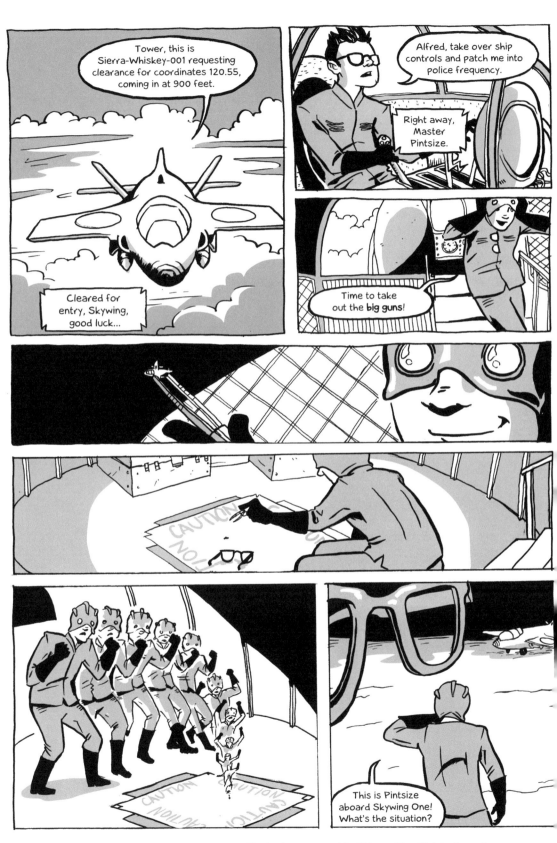

In case there were any doubts about whether Pintsize is great or not, just let me affirm, Pintsize is great.

This is Badge. Cleaver's in a courtyard with Mega Girl on 12th between 5th and 6th, we're stationed down the block locking down on F-men.

You can't arrest me! I'm a superhero too!

How come I never heard of you?

... I'm on my way.

Copy that, Pintsize. I'm ready to engage if you need me.

Officer!

Negative. No offense, Badge, but this is a fight I'm not even sure Mega Girl can win.

What is it?

I'm the kid's fire-chief, is she alright, what's going on in there?

Whose fire chief?

Alison Green!

Mega Girl? She and Cleaver are talking. If shit goes down, trust me, we'll all notice.

Bullets, tank shells, even you couldn't give me much more than a black eye.

But my arms got so sharp, now I cut myself without even trying.

So I figure that means I can slice you up real good too. Don't you think?

Not everyone with superpowers fights crime, and not everyone who fights crime has superpowers.

For all those smart alecs out there, those shorts were made by the Federal Government when Cleaver was first put in prison.

Alfred is the name of the Skywing's computer.

And Pepper is the name of the Nucleus's computer. Pintsize is such a NERD!

Alison has heard some iteration of this joke from Pintsize probably a thousand times.

For the squeamish amongst our readers, that bus had already been evacuated.

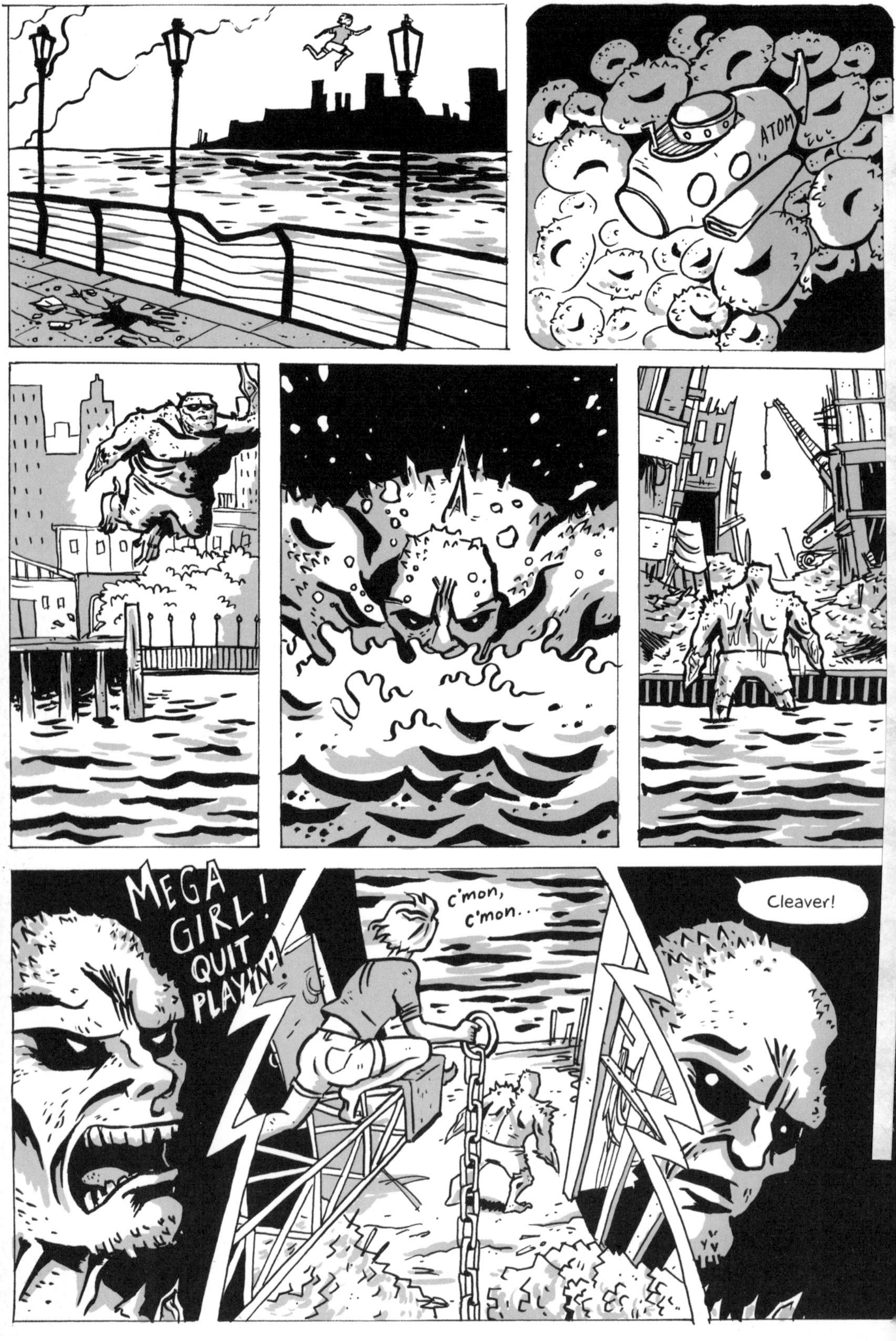
ATOM
MEGA GIRL! QUIT PLAYIN'!
c'mon, c'mon...
Cleaver!

Alison Green jump good.

I just love strange teamwork.

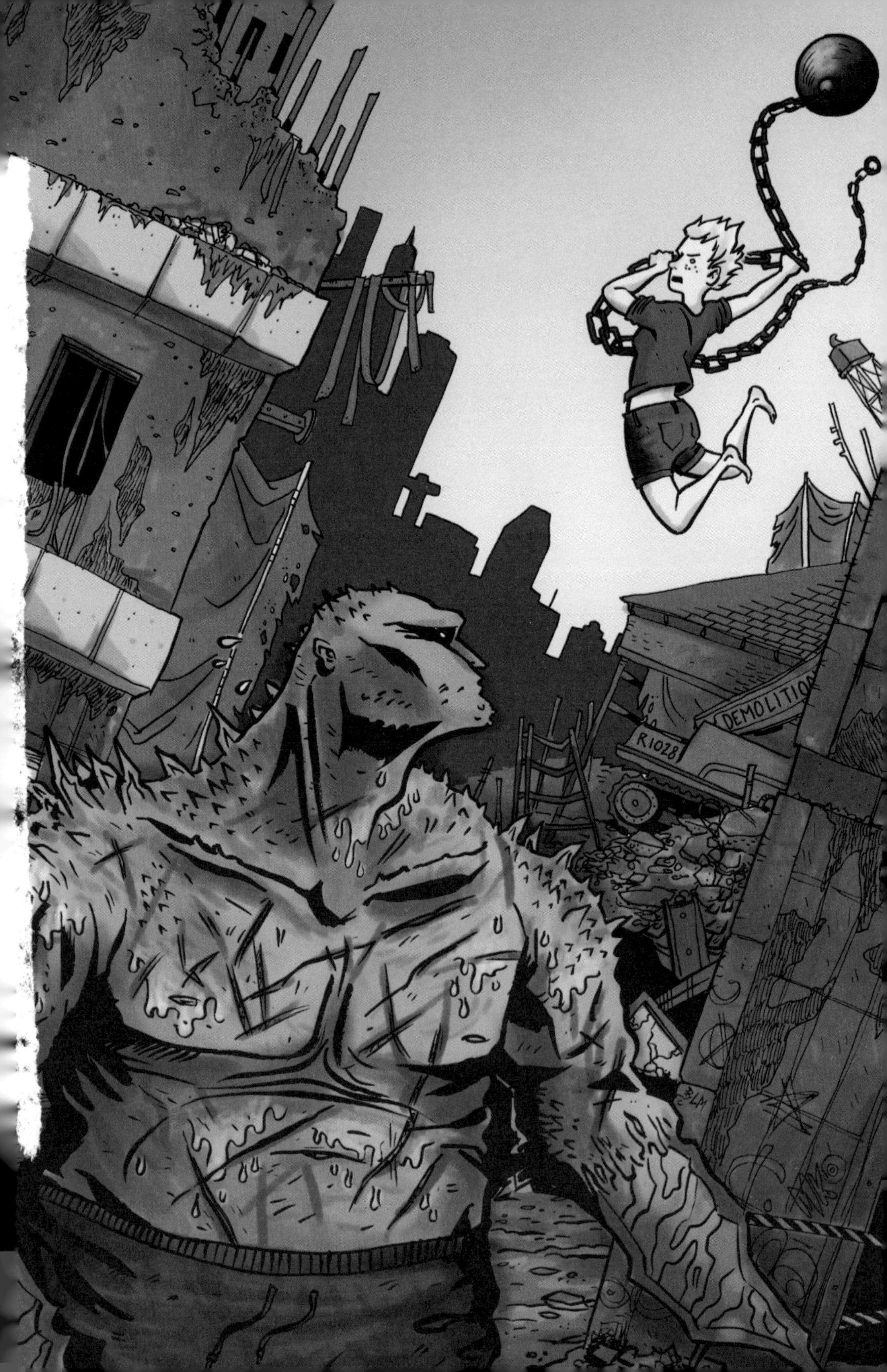
DEMOLITIO
R1028

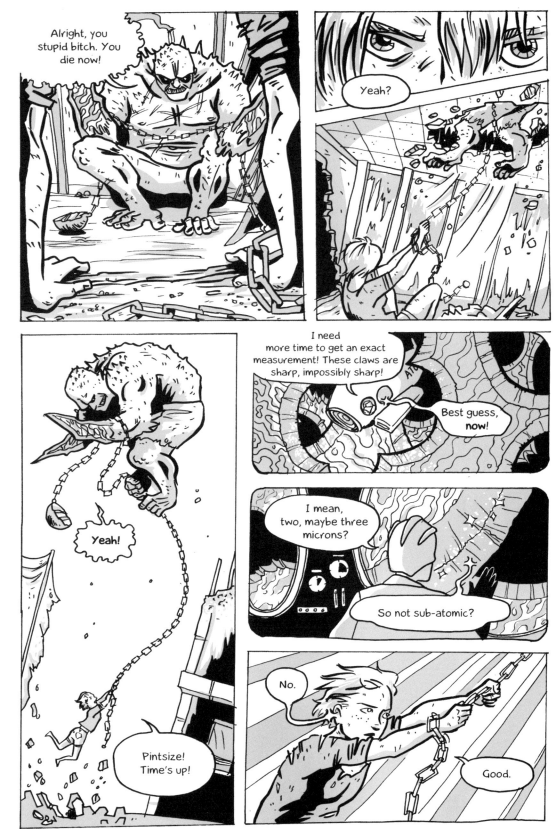

Worth pointing out that Alison's super-strength and Cleaver's are generated by different biodynamic effects. Alison is an autonomic somadynamic, whereas Cleaver is a muscular, dermal, and osteodynamic savant. Pintsize can shrink real small!!

YANK

My turn.

Nnngggh...

Now don't pass out just yet.

Alison?
Alison!?
Hello!?

Alison is a scary lady.

Let me clear something up for you.

First, you gotta be as dumb as you look if you think you're the only one on the planet whose powers have been getting worse.

Second... You think I don't want to fight anymore?

I **love** fighting. I love the blood, I love the heat, I love breaking shit. It's the only thing I've ever been good at, and the fact that it never makes anything better **just fucking kills me.**

Please... stop... can't...

So tell your friends. Any time they wanna go, I'm ready. Nothing makes me happier, nothing makes more sense to me, than kicking the shit out of people like you.

Uggghhhhh...

Invincible or not, you still gotta breathe.

You've seen this photograph before, page 25 of this very issue.

Theodore Cohen and Marcus Housten were never married, but they were very much in love from 1979 to 2008.

That concussion is not getting any better because of this flashback/obituary/epiphany hybrid.

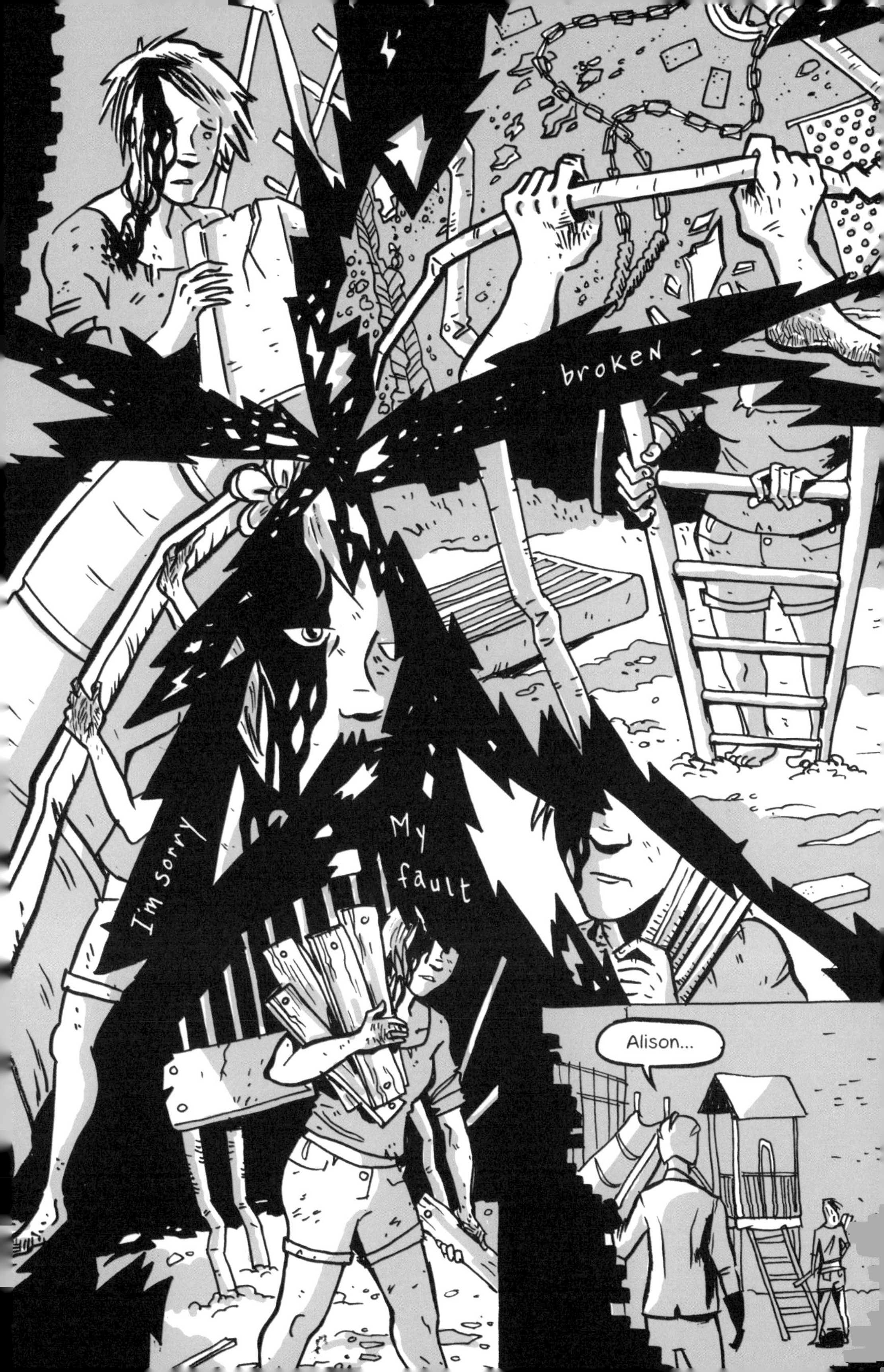
broken
I'm sorry
My fault
Alison...

Pro Tip: if you want to get someone to cry, subtly mock them while they're sick with guilt and doing the best they can.

Bacon, egg n' cheese and a big ol' coffee! Official Breakfast of The Guardians!

Thanks, Pintsize.

How's it feel getting cut for the first time?

... Weird. I mean, I've felt pain before, but... it was weird.

You didn't let it stop you.

No, I guess I didn't.

They've got Cleaver somewhere secret, Max Security, they're not keeping him with other Bios anymore.

Hm.

How'd you know he wouldn't be able to cut past your bones?

Didn't. Dr. Rosenblum said she thought the molecular structure of my bone was probably stronger than my skin, based on... Well, whatever, I knew I wasn't gonna be able to get close to Cleaver without him getting a swing in, so I just wanted to make sure he didn't have some telekinetic aspect to his arms is all.

That said, his arms were **definitely** sharper than three microns across.

I told you I needed more time for the measurements!!

What You Missed: the bodega owner wouldn't take Pintsize's money, so he shrunk down and slipped it into the cash register while he wasn't looking.

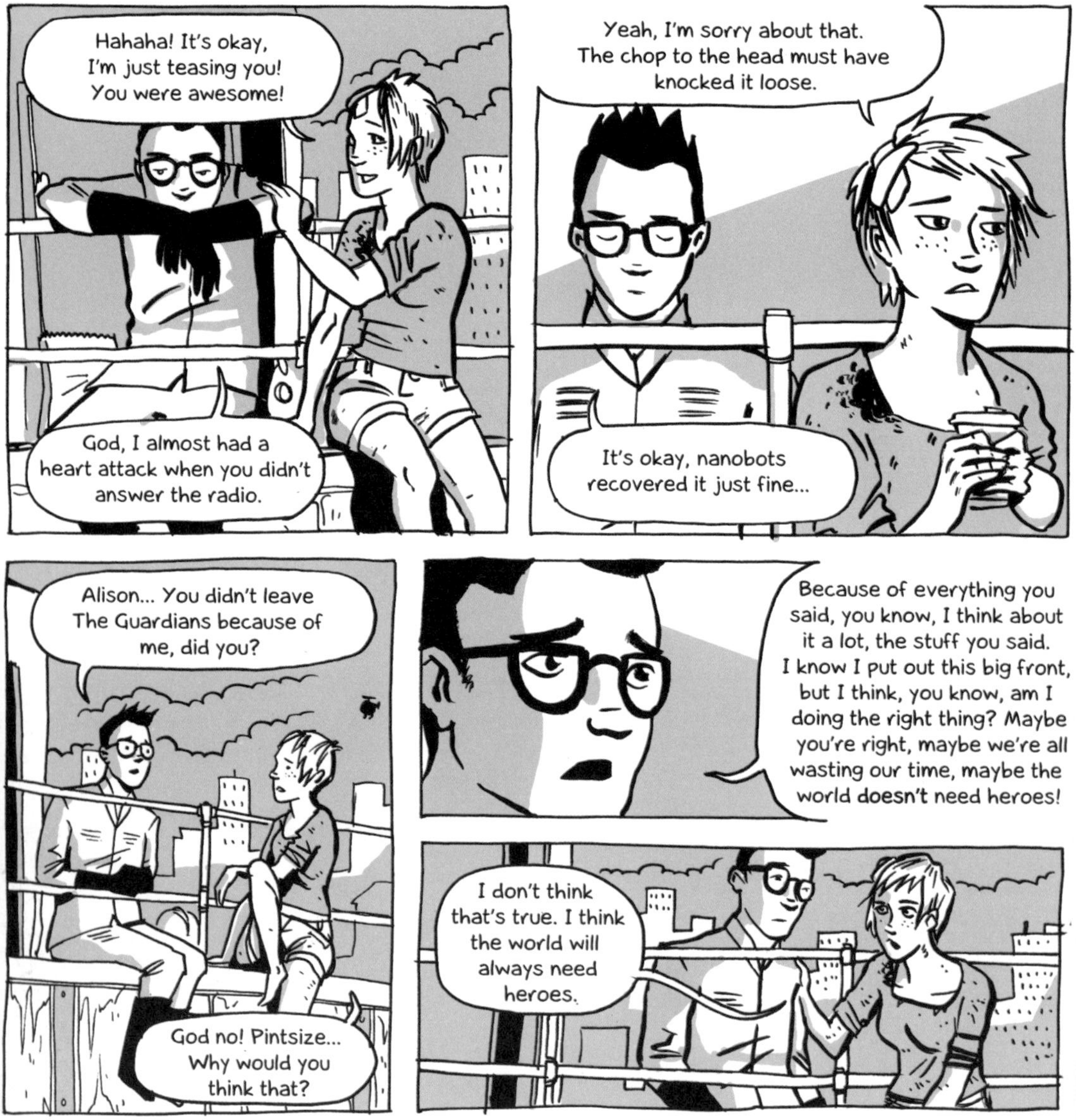
Hahaha! It's okay, I'm just teasing you! You were awesome!
God, I almost had a heart attack when you didn't answer the radio.
Yeah, I'm sorry about that. The chop to the head must have knocked it loose.
It's okay, nanobots recovered it just fine...
Alison... You didn't leave The Guardians because of me, did you?
God no! Pintsize... Why would you think that?
Because of everything you said, you know, I think about it a lot, the stuff you said. I know I put out this big front, but I think, you know, am I doing the right thing? Maybe you're right, maybe we're all wasting our time, maybe the world **doesn't** need heroes!
I don't think that's true. I think the world will always need heroes.

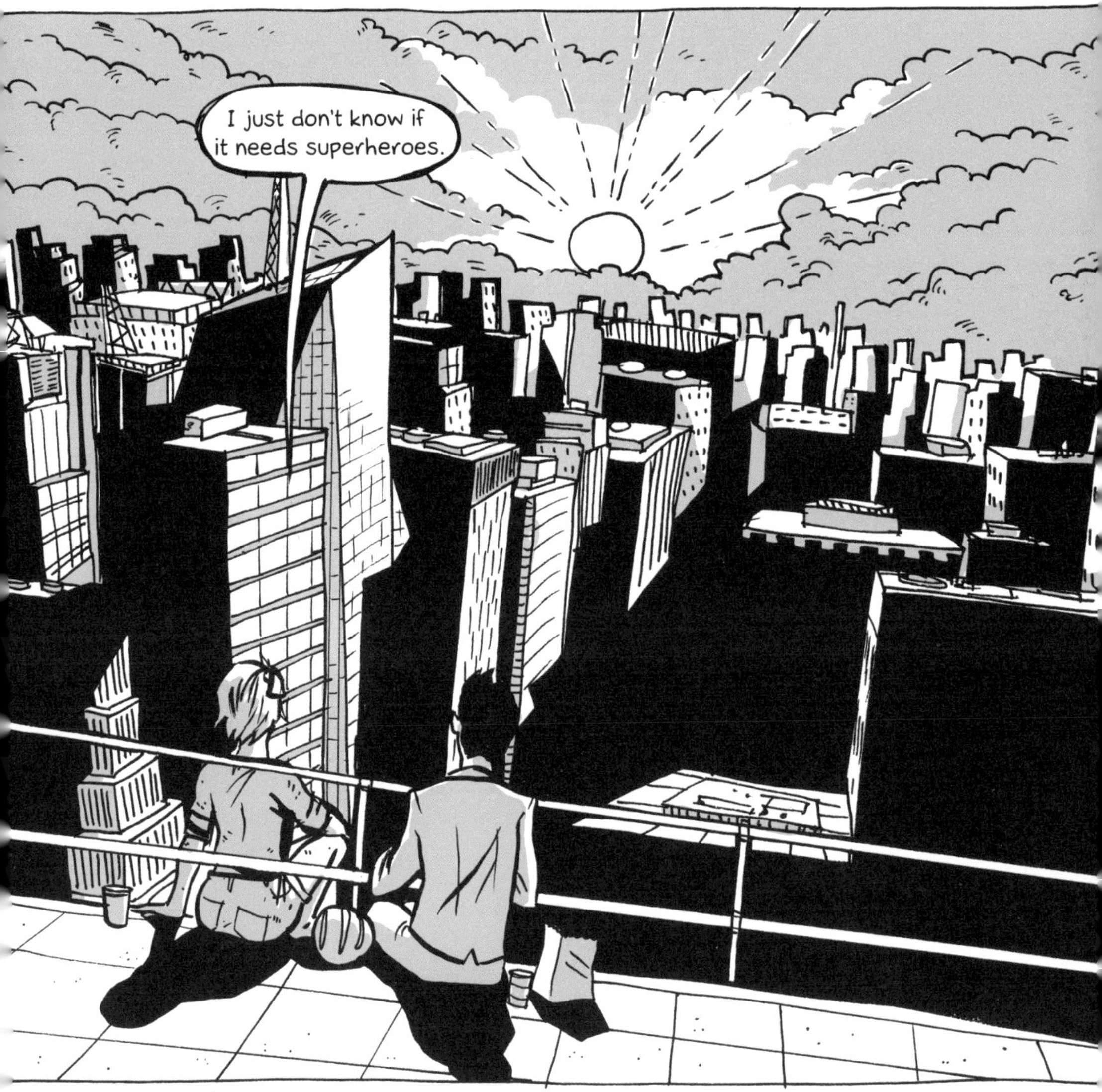
I just don't know if it needs superheroes.

New York is a good city.

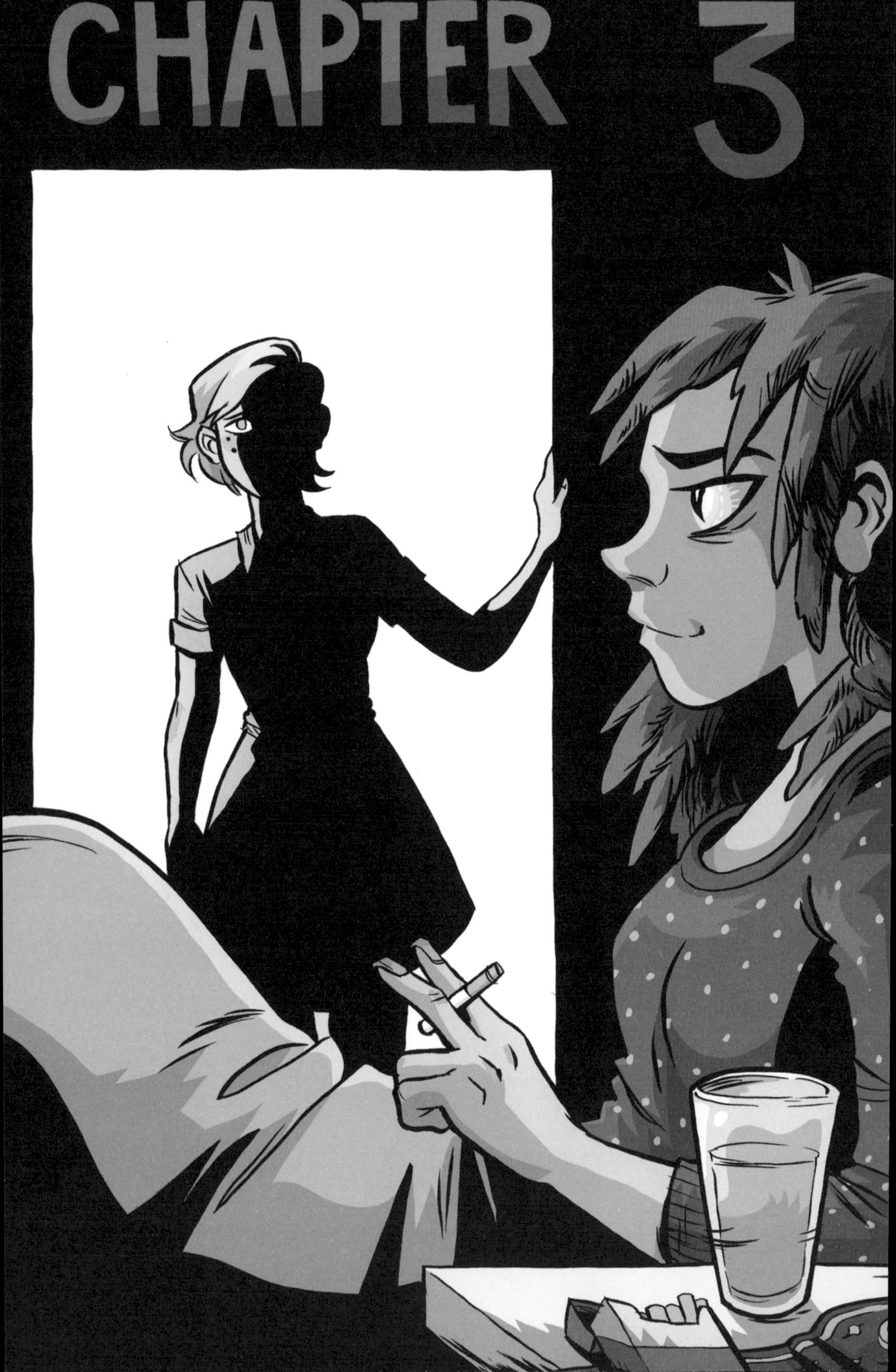
CHAPTER 3

It will continue to fade over time, but I'm afraid it will always be there. Without the ability to stitch or staple the injury, there's little we could do to prevent scarring.

Fine by me! Hopefully this was all helpful to you.

Extremely helpful! Studying your first injury will certainly yield some new insights into your anomaly.

I'll have to write Cleaver a thank you note.

You'll have to write it soon, his condition is worsening rapidly.

What do you mean?

Well, Cleaver's anomaly is technically a form of cancer. Those crystalline blades on his body are metastatized cancer cells and from what we can gather, he has many more internal protrusions than external.

... Is it going to kill him?

Eventually, I should hope so. It will be a very painful life if it doesn't.

Superpowers are not always fun and games and smashing things.

So I got automatically passed in all my classes for the semester, and the school's shut down for the next week or two while they fix everything.

What are you going to do with the time off, do you know?

I thought about going home for a bit. I've sort of cleaned up as much debris as possible, everything else I should really leave to the experts.

Hm...

What's up?

No, no! Nothing at all!

Oh dear! My new scar seems to have granted me the ability to read minds! I sense that you have something that you want to say!

Alright, I'll just come out and ask. Have you spoken to Feral recently?

Feral? I haven't seen Feral in years. Why do you bring it up?

For the record, the scar did not give her mind-reading powers, guys.

Hot Coffee, Mississippi, 2008

Louisa's

Why the hell are we working with these people!?

Mega Girl, we have to, we're not going to be able to shut down the reactor, free the test subjects, and stop Ignomino from escaping unless we accept what they're offering!

This is crazy! These people are wanted criminals! Feral's not a superhero, she's holding a gun, for God's sake!

How else you s'posed to shoot somebody?

Do you see what I'm saying?

Y'all about done? I was figuring on fighting some crime today, if we had the time.

Look, we're both trying to take out the Zenith Initiative. We can either work together, or get in each other's way.

Fine.

I agree, Mega Girl, guns are stupid.

Digger can bring you right up into that there cell block. Sonar and Snake bust 'em hostages out and haul ass back through the tunnel.

Meanwhiles, Moonshadow shoulda had all them gates open by then, so Crystal and Pintsize can shut down the reactor.

And Ignomino?

That's where me and you come in.

I can handle him by myself.

Aw, c'mon! It'll give us gals a chance to catch up!

It may actually be a good idea to have you set up at HQ, on the radio, Feral.

Whatever you say, fella. Y'all's the big New York City heroes, we just tryin' to keep up is all!

Can't we all just get along, gang?!

Red three... Move Out...

CRASH

Door was wide open, ya know.

In her defense, I probably wouldn't be that keen on doors, either.

Guys, regenerating is gross as hell.

God damn, that shit hurts!

Are you alright?

Who, me?

NEVER BEEN BETTER!

There's your man, Mega Girl!

Put on a shirt, Ignomino!

It was wrong of you to come here. You will be punished for your insolence.

RRRAAARR

Not so fast, Mega Girl.

THOK

Did you just throw a gun at me?

Fffug youu...

Hard to get your fingers around the trigger with a sword in your brain!

Alison has a mean fastball, guys.

You know all these people?

More or less. You got nothin' to worry about, darlin', they ain't payin' no attention to you.

Here's your root beer.

Thanks!

That was a killer move with your shoe, how'd you know to do that?

I got the idea from you throwing the pistol! I saw that Ignomino had to focus to use his telekinesis, and you had him distracted

We make a pretty good team.

I'll say! I was worried at first, but you're one badass lady, Feral!

If you're a superhuman in Hot Coffee, MS, get down to Louisa's for a good ol' time!

Feral!
Oh my God,
I am so sorry!
Are you okay?

nnngggghh...

Oh my God, I am so, so sorry...

CRICK

Damn, girl, how about a "No, thank you" next time?

Excuse me, **next time**? Look, I'm sorry I broke your limbs or whatever, but what you did was super rude!

You threw me through a window!

It was an accident! What you did was on purpose! Also, hi! I'm not interested in girls!

Well, I am!

Look, I really am sorry. I overreacted. I've never even been on a date with anyone, let alone kissed somebody, and I didn't think it would happen in a Biker Bar in Mississippi is all. I'm sorry.

... You think datin' comes **before** makin' out with somebody?

Please don't tell the world how uncool I am.

Don't worry, sugar, your secret's safe with me. But for Christ's sake, if I can't kiss ya, at least let me show ya how to relax...

Another turnoff was the whole regurgitation/regeneration deal.

Present Day

SENATE
BALCONY A

Hey! Do you want to go on a road trip with me? Also, hi!

For a refresher on who this jamoke is, check out issue one!

Don't worry, Patrick's not taking Alison to his secret underground lair, that's just the Holland Tunnel.

Mind if I put some music on?

Go right ahead. I'd prefer anything without lyrics, if that's okay.

Why not lyrics?

It's... well, it's just very distracting. Hearing a human voice disconnected from their thoughts is jarring for me. It's like if someone didn't use nouns in their sentences.

That's a bad analogy, I apologize. Here, it's like if you'd only ever watched movies with the Director's Commentary, and then you were forced to watch an old silent film.

That actually sounds kind of nice...

Wait, can you watch movies?

Honestly, they really stress me out.

Ha! So, what, you just see plays?

The play is never as interesting as the audience, I'm afraid.

Patrick could probably drive blindfolded alongside that many other drivers.

It's kind of like a sense of hearing. I can ignore some noises and focus on others up to a point, but I can never really shut it down. Even when I'm asleep, my telepathy is still operating.

Well I'm sorry to hear that. Not that you'd want to, but could you find a way to turn it off?

So what you're saying is, you're constantly reading my mind?

Yes. I'm sorry if that makes you uncomfortable.

Why would **you** reading **my** mind make **me** uncomfortable?

I don't...

Please stop...

Ahahahaha!

Gotcha!

Alright, I'll stop.

But I think you should have to tell me a secret about yourself, to make it fair that you can read my mind.

A secret about me, huh? Hm...

Alright, here's one. I have never been able to mind control anybody, at any time, ever.

What!? That can't... How is that true? I mean, I know that some people lied about being mind-controlled by you, like that guy who worked at Citibank...

They all lied. I'm sure it'd be very useful to take over a person's body like a marionette, but I wouldn't know, for I am but a humble mind-reader.

But if...

Wouldn't you? Look, it's simple...

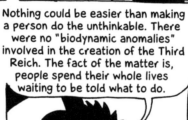

Nothing could be easier than making a person do the unthinkable. There were no "biodynamic anomalies" involved in the creation of the Third Reich. The fact of the matter is, people spend their whole lives waiting to be told what to do.

The idea that I would need mind control to get people to do what I need them to is, frankly, insulting. If you can hear someone's darkest desire, and see their entire memory laid out in front of you, and you still can't get them to do what you'd like, it says more about you than the people you're attempting to control.

YOU ARE SO SPOOKY!

I heard you the first time.

Oh man, Freeze Ray Ice Cream!! THE BEST!

There's a rest stop in a few miles.

Oh!... Thank you.

Ugh, I hate fast food.

No you don't.

Could you just cool it with the mind-reading for a second?

Sorry, yes, I agree, I also hate fast food. That's why we both ordered it and are now eating it.

Let me have my little throwaway statements, you telepathic jerk!

Hey! I know you already know this, but I really appreciate you coming on this trip with me. It's nice to finally spend some time with you, not just exchanging emails or getting coffee once in a while.

Are you Mega Girl!?

Heather! She ain't a superhero no more!

I couldn't agree more. I have to admit, if you had told me this time last year that "Mega Girl" would be my best...

I'm so sorry to bother you, Miz Green, it's just you're Heather's favorite, and she hasn't never seen a superhero before!

No, no, that's okay! In New York, everyone's kind of over superheroes, so this is a real treat!

You're the best hero! I always play you at recess and beat up the bad guys!

Aw, cool! I bet you're a great hero!

What's your name?

Heather!

Well my name's Alison, and this is a good luck quarter, to help you fight bad guys.

Heather is such a cutie-pie! That's probably why Alison said 'Aw, Cool!' instead of taking an hour and a half to talk through the ethical ramifications of violence and the inherant flaws in the concept of 'superheroism'.

Aaaaaaagh! So Cool!

Just make sure to always listen to your Mom!

I really can't thank you enough for this. It means the world to her. It means so much.

Oh... It's no problem at all, just 25 cents, haha!

Run on back and finish your french fries!

Thank you Thank you Thank you!

She's so cute!

Miz Green... Heather's daddy was a policeman. He was killed by Menace.

Oh my...

Please be a superhero again. It's too late for my husband, but it would mean so much to...

I'm so sorry, Miss. I'm so sorry for your loss, I have to go.

Please, Miz Green! Menace is still out there somewhere!

...Momma?

In her mind, Alison is crossing "eating at highway rest areas" off the increasingly small list of normal things she can do.

Hey, do you ...

Shall I save us a 45 minute conversation?

I'm not a supervillain anymore. I can't prove it in a way you couldn't doubt, but it's true. As childish as you think it is to be a superhero, I am that much more disdainful of "villainy," super or otherwise.

I don't know who's manipulating my old criminal network. I can only tell you that when I find them, I'm going to kill them, though not before I've scoured their memory for every person who has ever helped them.

What I am doing with my time is running several large corporations. I invest a lot of time reading the minds of brilliant and important people. I'm still searching for answers to the same questions I had when you broke down my wall and threw me into a table.

And regarding that woman at Flashburger, she found her husband in the closet with his pants around his ankles and a bag over his head. I'd blame mind-control too.

... Patrick, are you a good person?

I don't really identify as a person... but I am trying very hard to do good things.

Alison is not sure what to do with this.

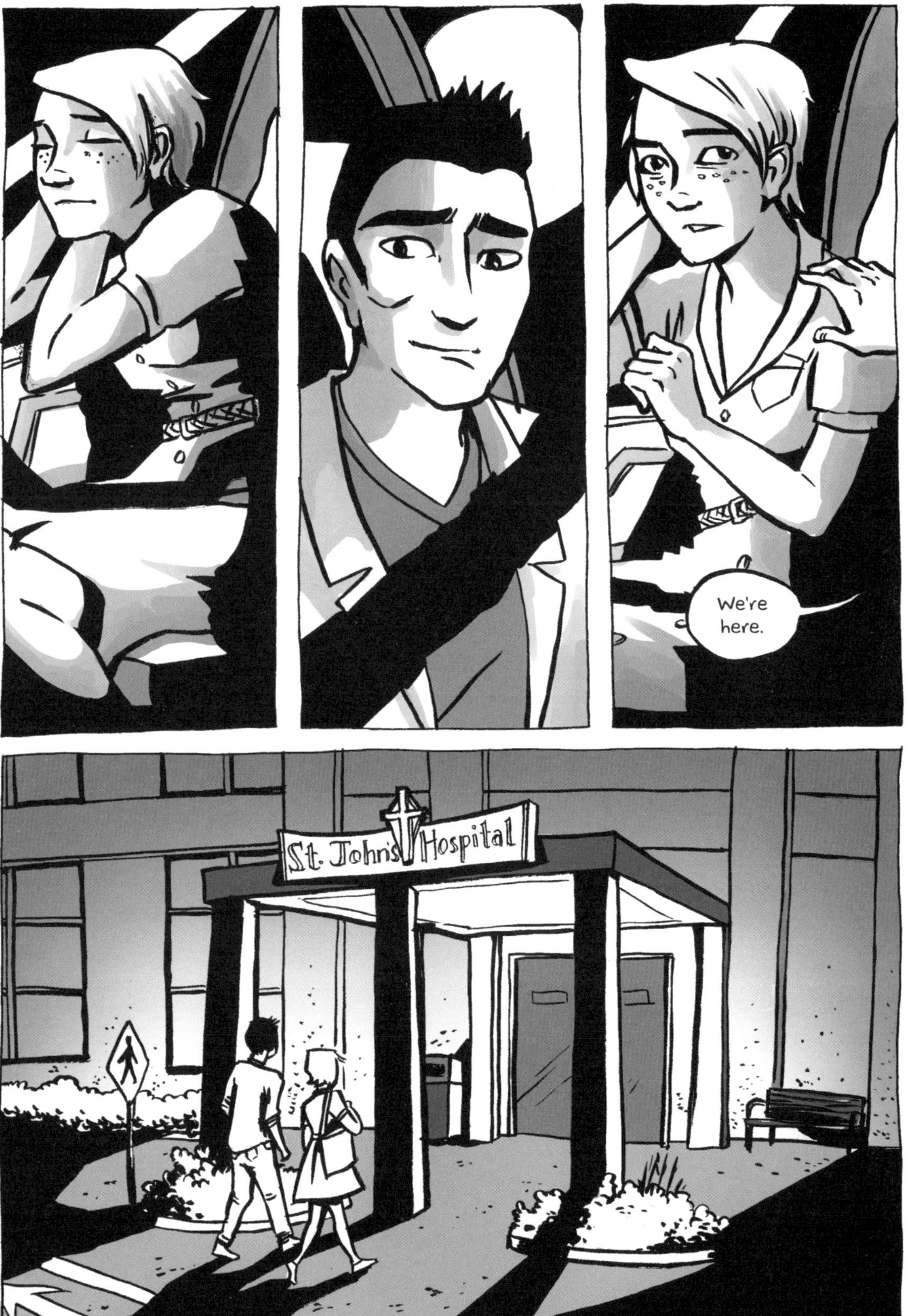
We're here.
St. John's Hospital

Patrick is either experiencing an emotion in panel two, or looking at something bittersweet Alison is dreaming. YOU DECIDE!!

Oh yeah, Feral's famous too! Infamous, really...

Well, I definitely could have handled that better... Probably the hospital's stress ball anyway...

Alison ...

Following our arrival here, I have become aware of a great deal of relevant and secret information. It would be of immense interest to you, but would invade the privacy of the person you've come here to see.

It's a secret of Feral's?

In a sense. She plans on telling you some but not all of it. I may have already overstepped some boundaries by telling you this much, but the ethics of privacy are troublesome for me to navigate.

It's okay. Thank you for checking in with me instead of just blurting it out. I know this has gotta be weird for you.

Never weird, just new.

... I think if Feral's gonna tell me, I should just let her tell me.

Understandable. I'll go check us in at the hotel.

'Kay. See you in a bit.

It was actually that woman's personal stress ball from home. Why am I telling you this? Because you have a right to know!

Hi, Feral...
Oh, were you asleep?

Hey, sugar.
Nah, it's okay,
come right in.

I'm sorry to
wake you up, it's really
good to see you.

It's good to
see you too. Been
a while!

Yeah, a few years
now... A hospital's not the
first place I would have
expected to find you.

You'd be surprised.
Lots a cute girls
is nurses, I shoulda
come to a hospital
sooner.

CLIK

How do
I look?

Fucking
terrible, actually.

Really?
You don't think I
could even play
the "feel sorry
for me" angle?

...Wait a second,
what am I asking
you for? You a
damn nerd!

No argument
here.

Yeah...
although I do smell
a man on you.

Hahahaha!

She can also tell you ate at Flashburger, which is maybe even more embarrassing.

Aw, you blushing on account of him?

Nope, just general embarrassment - blushing.

So tell me about him.

He got prettier eyes than me?

Feral... I need to know what's going on.

Aw, dang. We done flirtin' already?

My doctor in the DBRD said she hardly knew anything. She told me you'd revealed your identity, that the Governor had pardoned you, and that I could find you here. At first I thought maybe Crystal was sick, or...

Crystal's been dead for a while now.

I'm so sorry. Please tell me what happened.

Oh. I had no idea...

It's okay. It happened right around when you took the mask off, you probably didn't read about it.

An unscrupulous hospital custodian has a fat stack of cash in his back pocket, both for disarming the smoke detector and buying the cigarettes in the first place.

After Ignomino got put away, and we said our goodbyes to all y'all, things got pretty bad for the Wild Ones.

Crystal started getting back into drugs, saying it helped her powers and whatnot.

Digger ended up going to jail for killin' them two judges in Jasper County.

Snake never really had much in the way of powers, he was workin' as a bouncer in Tampa last I heard from him.

Just keep running

When the Wild Ones started falling apart, I started falling apart too.

Fucked about any girl I could get my hands on, killed people just for sayin' shit I didn't wanna listen to.

Sometimes I'd just start laughin' for no reason.

I figured out it's cause I wanted to die, but I wasn't smart enough to figure out how to actually do it.

Louisa's

I was trying to figure out why winning felt so damn much like losing...

Then you took that little mask off...

and running.

Those two guys in the bar are gossiping about how upset they are that they're only ever going to appear as side characters in Feral's story.

By "England and France and Places" Feral is of course referring to Europe.

You can convey a lot with black and white and grey, but you should probably know that the guy on the right in the first panel has bright blue skin.

Change your shirt already, Feral!

HrRRrrKK!

Are you alright?

I'm fine...

Feral... I don't mean to interrupt your story... But I'm really nervous.

The fact that you're coughing, I mean... That's not supposed to happen with someone with your anomaly.

You always were ready to dispose with the pleasantries, weren't ya?

I don't want to rush you, but I want to know if anything's wrong.

Far from it. Everything's great.

My whole point was, I learned a lot out there. And it was all thanks to you. So thank you.

If you don't mind, could we do the rest in the morning? I've got other people coming to visit me, and I'd like to give them time alone as well.

Of course. Get some rest...

Feral has coughed before, just mostly after she's been shot up, or had her throat cut, or breathed in a bunch of bees...

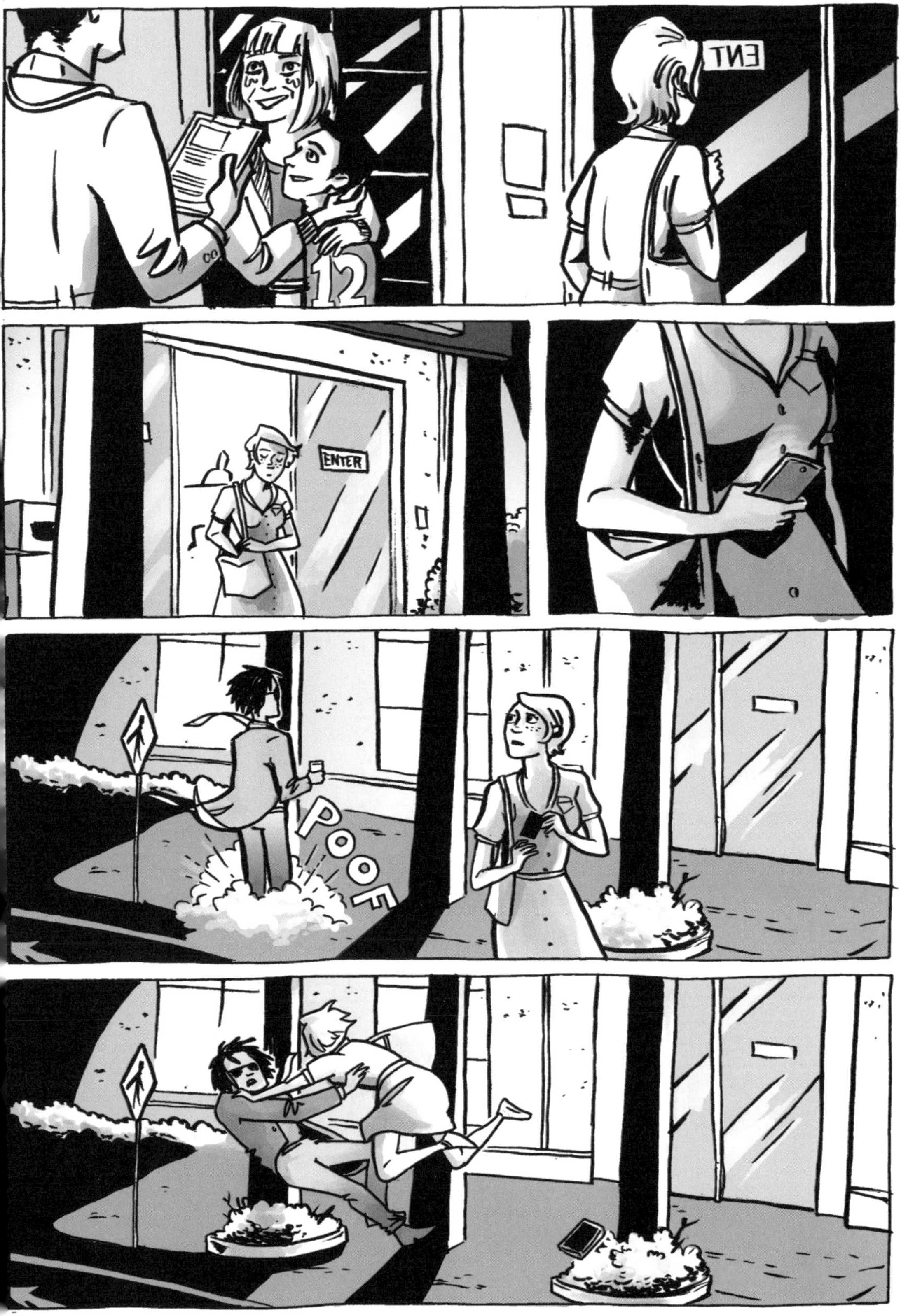

ENT
ENTER
12
POOF

GET 'IM!

POOF

Hold on a bloody moment! We mean you no harm, yeah?

Sorry, training kicked in. Never let a teleporter get a bead on the layout.

Oh, I recognize you. You're that Mega Girl, right?

The one who took the mask off and let slip the dogs of normalcy?

That would be me. Who are you?

Johnny Temple, naturally.

Oh, that's right. You're that teleporter who makes clothes?

I'm that fashion designer who can teleport, you mean to say.

Right. What are you doing here?

Payin' a visit to Ms. Feral, aren't I?

Sure, Johnny Temple is so cool he wears sunglasses at night. But really, the concept of 'at night' is pretty loose for a guy who can be in any time zone at any moment.

How do you know her?

We met at a loft party when she was havin' a go at a model friend of mine back in autumn.

She kipped with me for a few weeks, before she up and vanished.

Did she...

POOF

That's distracting.

Just trying to be a good host, there's a party on at my flat in Islington.

As I was saying, Feral's the genuine article. We got along like legends, ran roughshod over the streets of London, and had a bloody fabulous time. She talked about you plenty.

I lost track of her 'round when spring started. You know anything I don't?

You know more than me, man.

I wouldn't write yourself off. The lady of the house spoke about you a great deal, seemed to care what you thought quite a bit.

Seems sort of bizarre that you two would get along.

Yeah?

He just grabbed that scotch out of somebody's surprised hands.

Patrick, I think you're confused. You said you were going to the hotel, but now I see you're on some sort of dock. Patrick! ...Patrick?

Gentlemen! Thank you for coming out of your way to meet with me.

New York would have been ill-advised with all the recent scrutiny.

It is hardly out of the way for us, Mr. Duval.

And thank you as well for your promptness and... how do you say, discretion in this matter.

As you requested.

And here you are in return.

CLOSED

A pleasure, Mr. Duval. It is of great importance to the members of the Harmony Council that Templar Industries has found such dynamic new leadership, especially after such a tumultuous period.

Agreed, Mr. Xu. Menace is no more, and now bygones can be bygones. Will you be heading to the airfield right away?

My colleagues will be flying back, but I'm afraid I do not have the time for such luxuries. Farewell.

Superspeed is not AS convenient as teleportation, but it doesn't go 'poof' either.

How'd I do?

I'll let you know if your performance wavers.

Driver, take me back to my car.

Alison Green

Sorry, got trapped in a conference call, on my way now. Do you want me to get some Freeze Ray for later?

Quickly.

Patrick...

Very well.

Patrick wants to talk to Alison, but SOMEONE'S gotta make sure that delicious Freeze Ray Ice Cream doesn't melt.

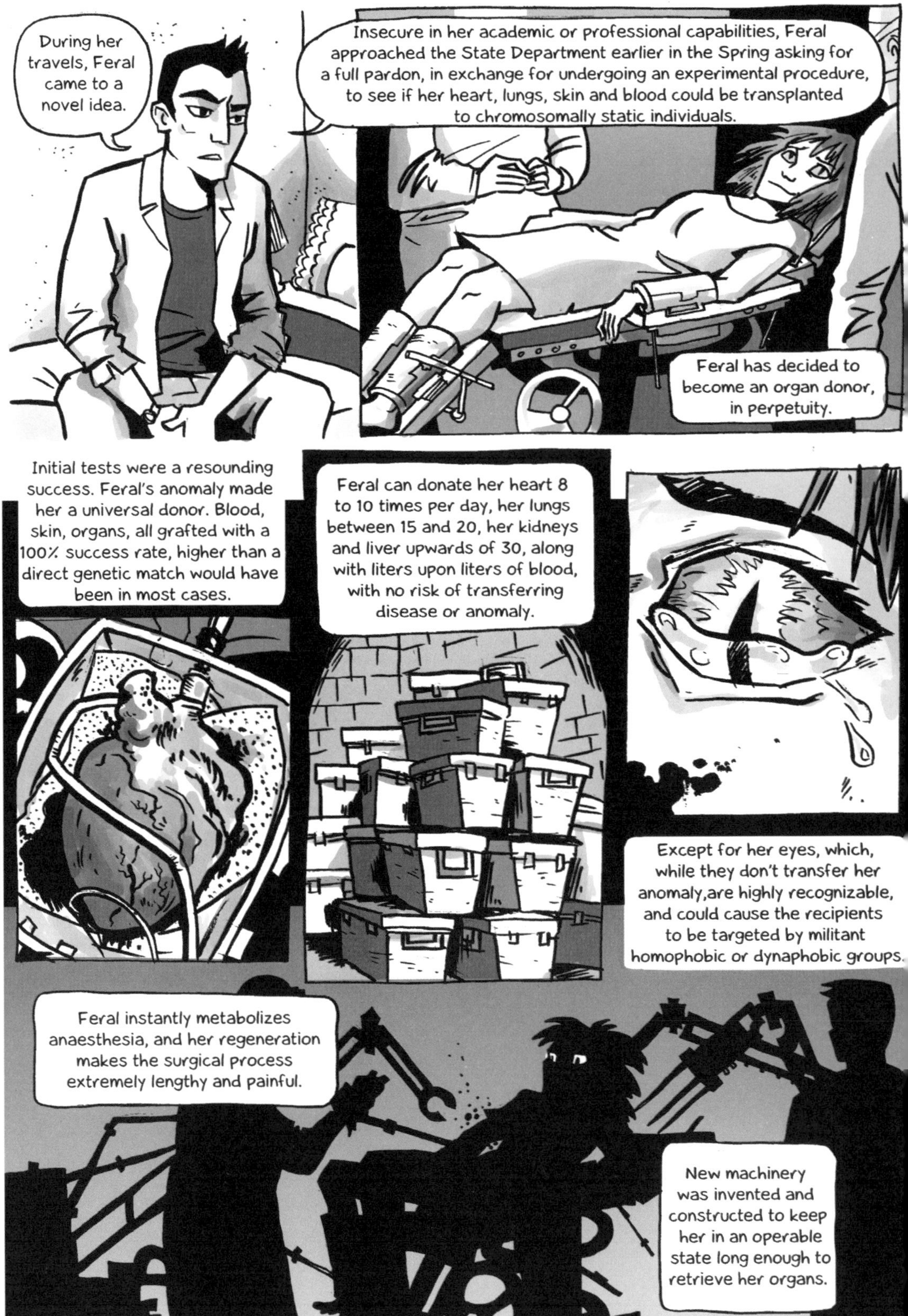

During her travels, Feral came to a novel idea.
Insecure in her academic or professional capabilities, Feral approached the State Department earlier in the Spring asking for a full pardon, in exchange for undergoing an experimental procedure, to see if her heart, lungs, skin and blood could be transplanted to chromosomally static individuals.
Feral has decided to become an organ donor, in perpetuity.
Initial tests were a resounding success. Feral's anomaly made her a universal donor. Blood, skin, organs, all grafted with a 100% success rate, higher than a direct genetic match would have been in most cases.
Feral can donate her heart 8 to 10 times per day, her lungs between 15 and 20, her kidneys and liver upwards of 30, along with liters upon liters of blood, with no risk of transferring disease or anomaly.
Except for her eyes, which, while they don't transfer her anomaly,are highly recognizable, and could cause the recipients to be targeted by militant homophobic or dynaphobic groups.
Feral instantly metabolizes anaesthesia, and her regeneration makes the surgical process extremely lengthy and painful.
New machinery was invented and constructed to keep her in an operable state long enough to retrieve her organs.

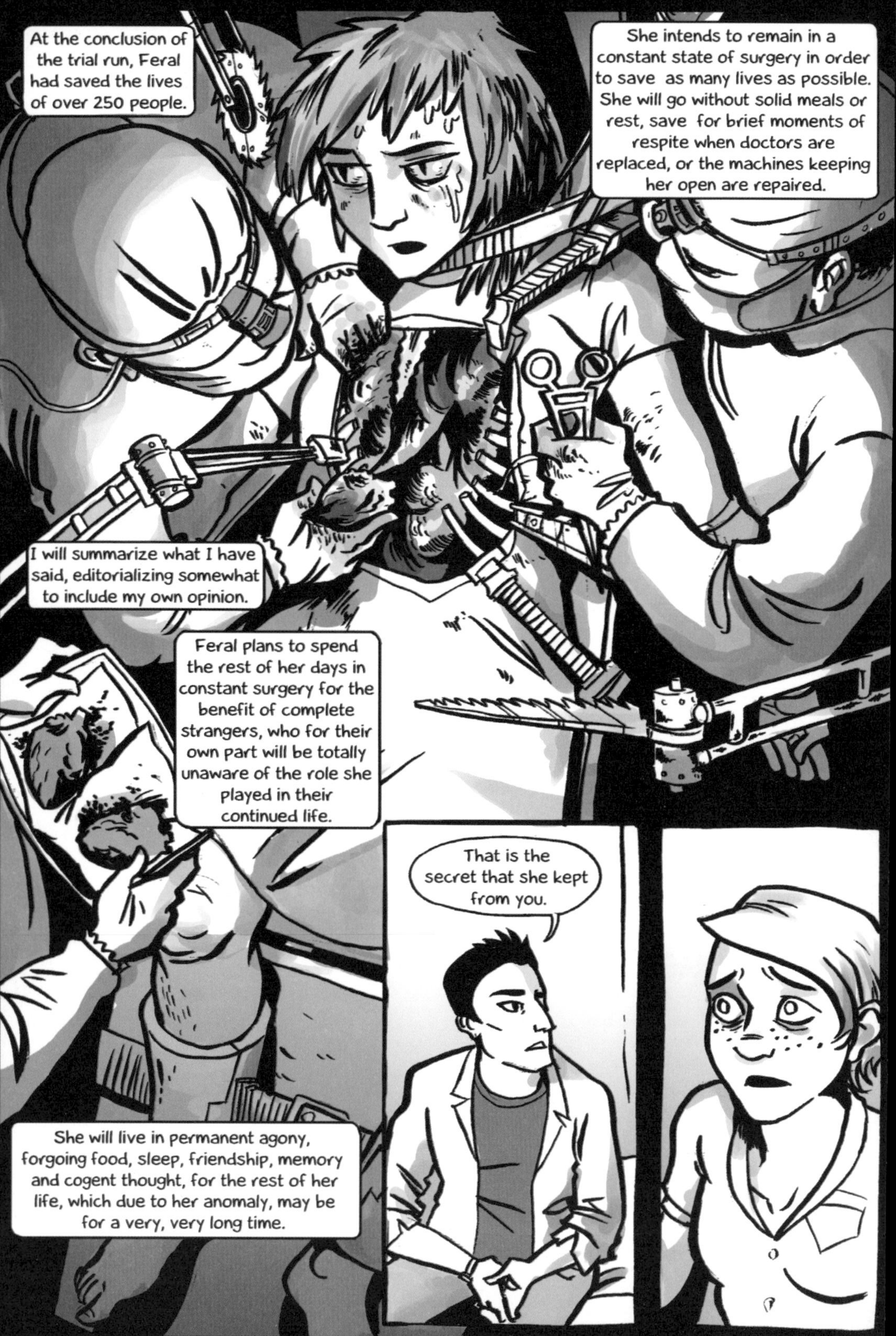
At the conclusion of the trial run, Feral had saved the lives of over 250 people.
She intends to remain in a constant state of surgery in order to save as many lives as possible. She will go without solid meals or rest, save for brief moments of respite when doctors are replaced, or the machines keeping her open are repaired.
I will summarize what I have said, editorializing somewhat to include my own opinion.
Feral plans to spend the rest of her days in constant surgery for the benefit of complete strangers, who for their own part will be totally unaware of the role she played in their continued life.
She will live in permanent agony, forgoing food, sleep, friendship, memory and cogent thought, for the rest of her life, which due to her anomaly, may be for a very, very long time.
That is the secret that she kept from you.

Meanwhile, a happy Midwestern family is having the time of their life in the hotel pool!

I mean, I've gotta stop her, right? That's the only thing I can do here. I'm not gonna let her go through with it, am I?

I have to do **something**!

You phrased most of those statements as questions.

Because it's all fucked, okay! It's the most heroic thing anyone has ever thought of doing!

She's doing it, on some level, because of stuff I said! And it will actually, genuinely save the lives of many, many people!

Why do I want to stop her? I can't want to stop her, she's a fucking... she's a superhero.

This is her decision. Right? Her horrifying, horrifying decision.

No. This is bad.

No, I should be okay with this.

Why am I not okay with this?

... You and I are alike in more than a few ways.

This page was guest written by Woody Allen (false).

Those freezers in mini-fridges don't always get the job done!

I'm still having a hard time figuring out what to say that will get her to stop.

Understandable. You're not manipulative. You're uncertain whether stopping her is morally correct or not.

These dilemmas are your kryptonite, so to speak.

Take it easy, **Lex**.

Pardon the reference.

Tomorrow, her responses to your points will generate new ideas to address in the moment. Until then, you should try to occupy your mind with something else.

Yeah...

Hey, what's the deal with Cleaver?

Dr. Rosenblum told me his armblades were cancer cells, does he know that?

Yes, he does. I provided a team of doctors for him when he was one of my primary...

...Henchmen?

...Perhaps.

I always referred to Daniel as an ally, but in retrospect, I suppose henchman is more descriptive.

His real name is Daniel?

Yes.

Probably good that the ice cream is a little melty, those plastic spoons are WORTHLESS.

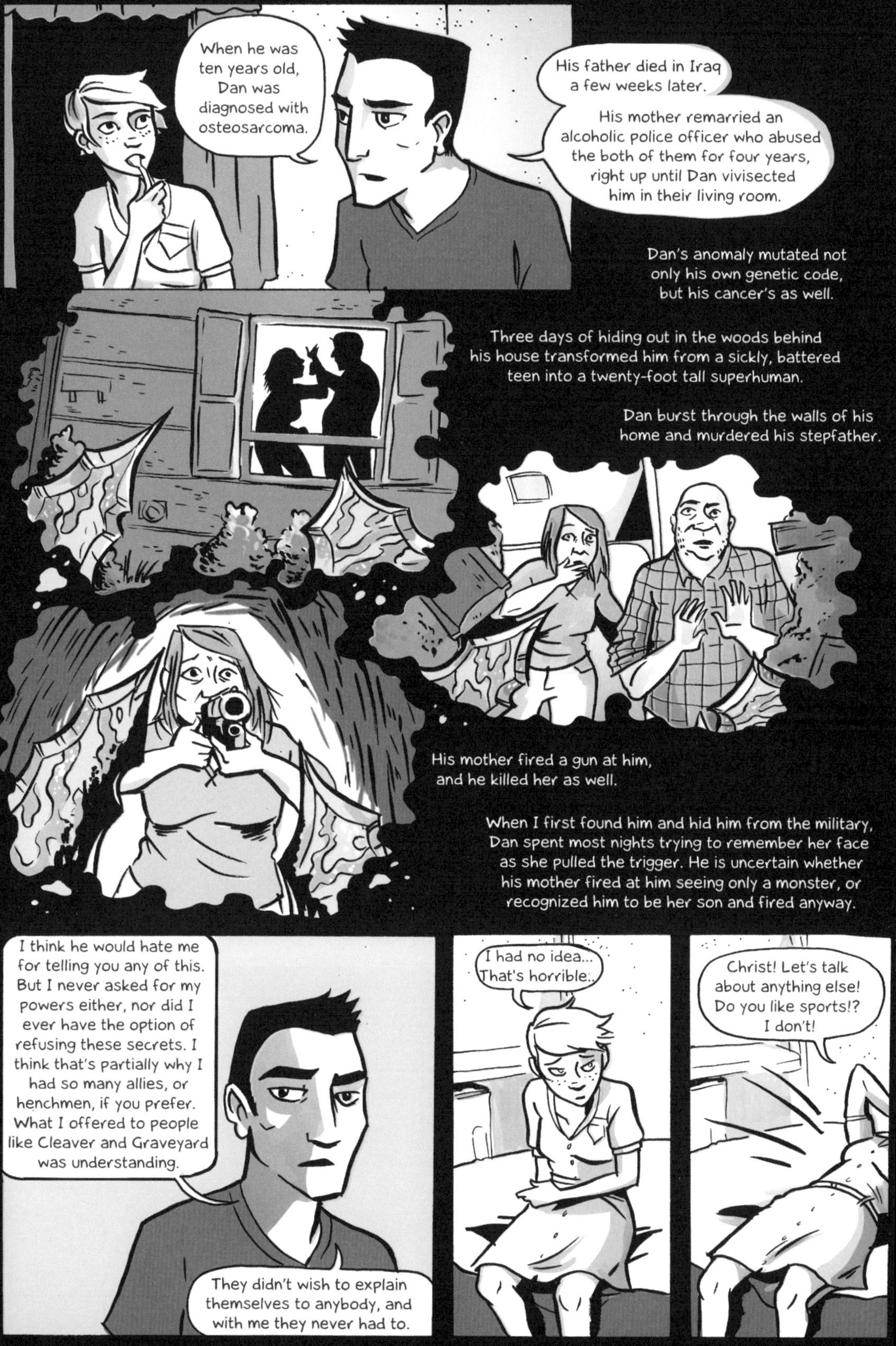
When he was ten years old, Dan was diagnosed with osteosarcoma.
His father died in Iraq a few weeks later.
His mother remarried an alcoholic police officer who abused the both of them for four years, right up until Dan vivisected him in their living room.
Dan's anomaly mutated not only his own genetic code, but his cancer's as well.
Three days of hiding out in the woods behind his house transformed him from a sickly, battered teen into a twenty-foot tall superhuman.
Dan burst through the walls of his home and murdered his stepfather.
His mother fired a gun at him, and he killed her as well.
When I first found him and hid him from the military, Dan spent most nights trying to remember her face as she pulled the trigger. He is uncertain whether his mother fired at him seeing only a monster, or recognized him to be her son and fired anyway.
I think he would hate me for telling you any of this. But I never asked for my powers either, nor did I ever have the option of refusing these secrets. I think that's partially why I had so many allies, or henchmen, if you prefer. What I offered to people like Cleaver and Graveyard was understanding.
They didn't wish to explain themselves to anybody, and with me they never had to.
I had no idea... That's horrible...
Christ! Let's talk about anything else! Do you like sports!? I don't!

Don't you know any happy secrets, Patrick?

Let's watch some TV!

Must we? I was serious on the trip, movies and television don't really sit well with me.

What about Loony Tunes? Those aren't really human beings, would that work for you?

Ugh, I don't know.

Have you ever seen them before?

Not firsthand.

Well, they're great. Let's give it a shot. What do you say?

Let's try that again.

I'll start it this time.

Okay.

Right.

Wabbit season!

Wabbit season!

Duck season.

Wabbit season!

...Wabbit season.

Duck season, FIRE!

BOOM

AHAHAHAHA HA

AHAHAHA HA

HA HA

This guy couldn't have been a supervillain, his laugh didn't start with a 'Mua!'

Patrick, are you going insane?

He... He just... He-he-he hee hee hee heeeeeeee!!!

CLICK

Hoooo! Oh my, I'm so sorry, I just, I justah-hahahahaha HAAA!

Tee-hee-hee! Daffy Duck's animosity towards the Bugs Bunny character is so intense, that he fails to see when Bugs has presented him an opportunity for victory!

Instead of...of maintaining an awareness of the words being used, Daffy's rage is so blinding that he frames his statements in pure contrariness to Bugs', which results in his getting **shot in the face!**

AHAHA!

Had he been less angry, he might have acted on Bugs Bunny saying "rabbit season," but he too strongly conflated his desire to disagree with his opponent and his desire to defeat him!

And it was that very desire to disagree that prevented him from fulfilling his ultimate goal of outwitting Bugs Bunny, and in so doing saving himself from harm! The irony is staggering! AHAHAHAHAHAHAHA!

Might we turn it back on? I was enjoying it!

Sure! Are you gonna pass out and die if we do?

It will be a small price to pay!

Break it down for us, Patrick.

The-thuh-thuh-the-that's all folks!

Hee-hee-heeee! Goodness, that coyote cannot seem to catch a break!

These are great! Why aren't people thinking about these all the time?

Why when I walk down the street am I not being constantly bombarded by people remembering Loony Tunes?

I mean, the part where Wile E. Coyote pursues Road Runner over the cliff's edge, only to become aware midway through that what he's attempting is physically impossible, and through that awareness succumbs to gravity?

What a hilarious commentary on the power of the delusional optimist versus the pyrrhic correctness of the realist!

The obliviousness of the Road Runner in contrast to...

I should go.

In contrast to what? IN CONTRAST TO WHAT?

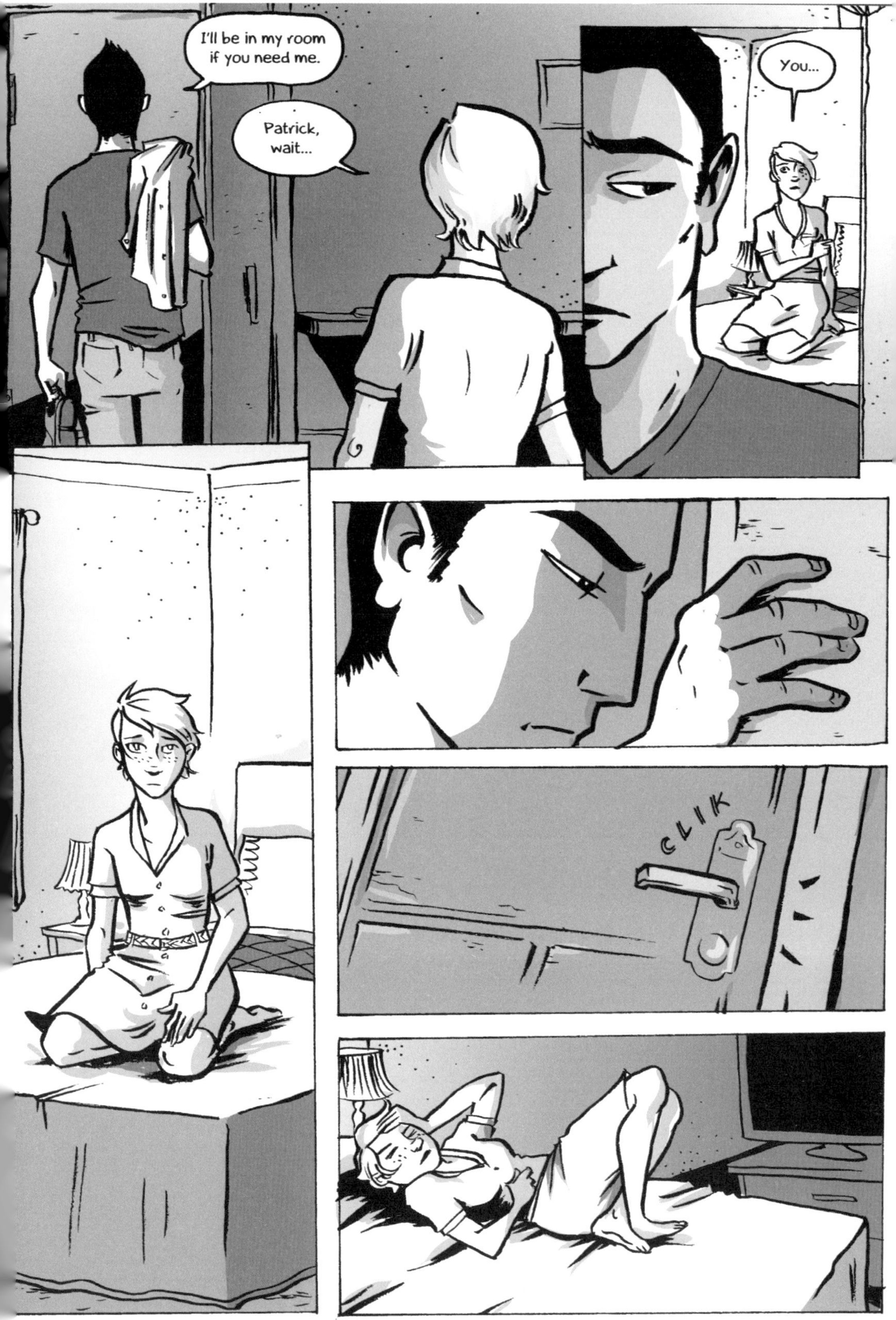

I'll be in my room if you need me.
Patrick, wait...
You...
CLIK

Not much to say, really.

Again, I am so, so sorry. The check is for the vending machine, if that is not enough, please email me and I will send you more, and I'm gonna go get some cash to pay for the candy right now.

Molly and Brennan have easily put more time and thought into the junk food branding of our superhero world than we have into some of our actual characters. Gotta get that candy right!

Communication is not Patrick's strong suit.

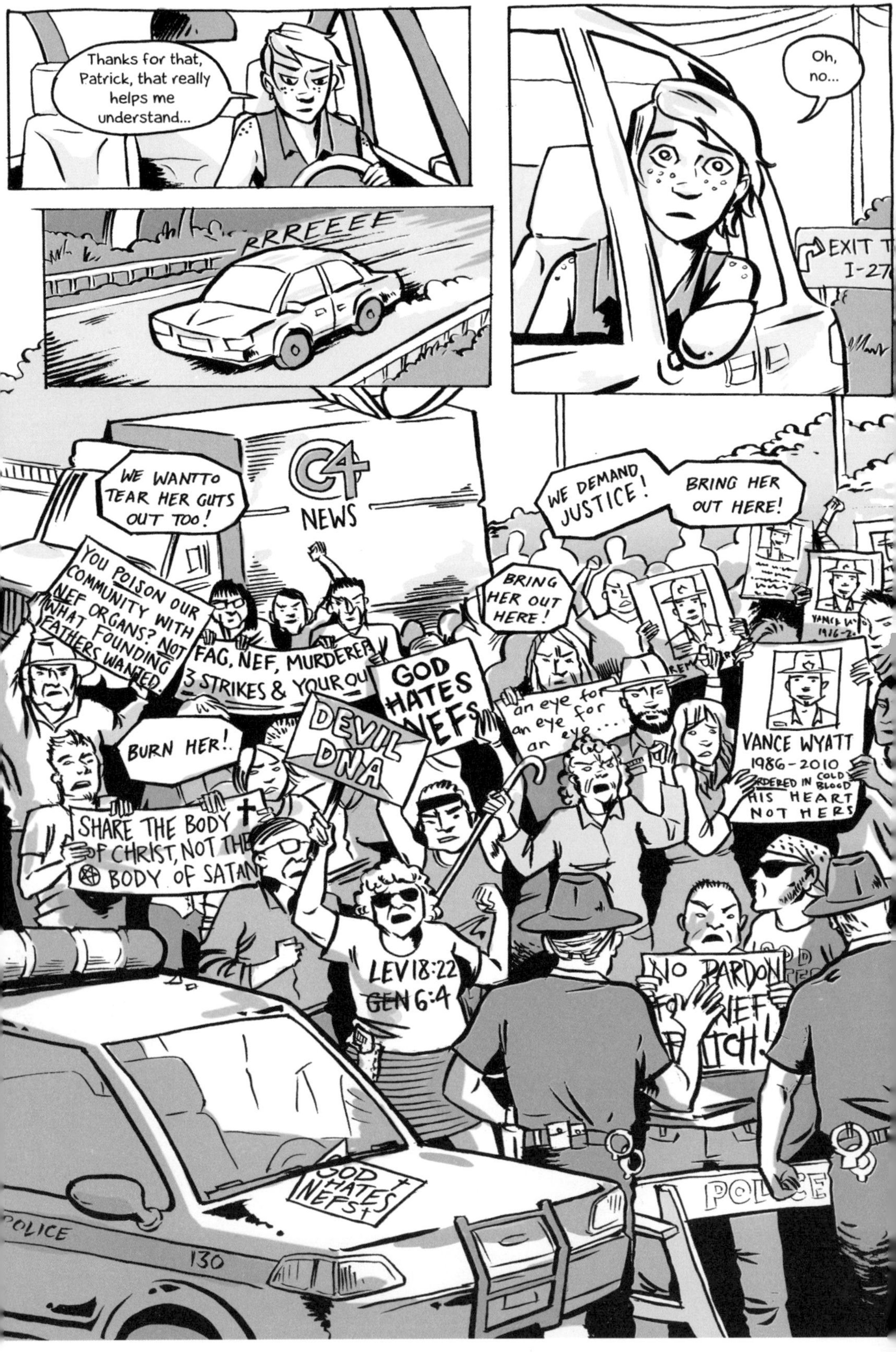
Thanks for that, Patrick, that really helps me understand...
RRREEEEE
Oh, no...
EXIT T
I-27
C4
NEWS
WE WANTTO TEAR HER GUTS OUT TOO!
WE DEMAND JUSTICE!
BRING HER OUT HERE!
BRING HER OUT HERE!
YOU POISON OUR COMMUNITY WITH NEF ORGANS? NOT WHAT FOUNDING FATHERS WANTED.
FAG, NEF, MURDERER
3 STRIKES & YOUR OU
GOD HATES NEFS
DEVIL DNA
an eye for an eye for an eye...
VANCE WYATT
1986-2010
RDERED IN COLD BLOOD
HIS HEART NOT HERS
BURN HER!
SHARE THE BODY OF CHRIST, NOT THE BODY OF SATAN
LEV 18:22
GEN 6:4
NO PARDON
GOD HATES NEFS
POLICE
130
POLICE

Trouble indeed.

BODY
T THE
SATAN

It's the Mega-Nef!

Look!

Go back where you came from!

SCREEE

Hey! What the hell is going on?

This is private property, right?

I'm sorry Ms. Green, is there a problem?

There's a huge, loud protest in front of a hospital! Aren't you going to arrest these people?

This isn't New York, Ma'am, we don't have the resources to hold 'em all.

Besides, they ain't hurtin' anybody. I woulda thought you of all people could appreciate a peaceful demonstration.

You've gotta be kidding me.

Feral...

I know.

Johnny Temple just heard the news.

There are multiple aspects to the whole superhero thing that Johnny doesn't really get.

You can tell Johnny is a fashionable guy, because watches are a purely aesthetic accessory even for a guy who CAN'T manifest in any time zone at any moment.

Look, you're absolutely right, okay? There are a lot of people who are happy to talk.

I'm not one of them. I'm still a firefighter, I still believe in taking action and doing what's right.

Good grief...

But this plan is so extreme, and so dangerous, and so... so crazy! You're going to torture yourself all day, every day, with no anaesthesia, for the rest of your potentially immortal life?

You said they'd designed a painkiller that worked!

And what's she on about with "all day"?

Alison, please stop...

What the bloody fuck!

You've gone completely up the fucking wall on this one, Tara!

Listen to me, please listen to me. You are beautiful, and wonderful, and one of a kind.

You did not ask for your powers, and you owe nothing to this world other than to be yourself and do what makes you happy.

Come stay with me in London, I can...

Johnny, I love you to pieces, but I can't stand the way you live.

And somethin' tells me you wouldn't much like Hot Coffee neither...

Why wouldn't you want to live with a guy whose t-shirt is that cool?!? Look at it! What is that, an eye with some lightning behind it? Classic cool!

Alison can really speak from the diaphragm when she wants to.

POOF

POOF

Stop!

Fighting!

I...I'm sorry I raised my voice.

But we can't just have a tiny fraction of people trying to save the world, a tiny fraction fucking it over, and everybody else just hanging out waiting to see what happens.

It's not sustainable.

I'm goin' through with the plan, and that's final.

It was never on the table to begin with, and your "advice" is unwelcome and unappreciated.

If you didn't want my advice...

Then why the **FUCK** did you invite me to come here!?

Because I think I probably love you.

And I wanted to say goodbye.

Ever notice how when you're extremely upset, everyone becomes bad at listening? Wonder what that's about...

All I have to do to stop you torturing yourself is to figure out how to stop bad things from happening? That's it?

Looks like this guy's had it as well.

The people who signed up for the experimental version of the procedure were told only
that a biodynamic anomaly had been involved.

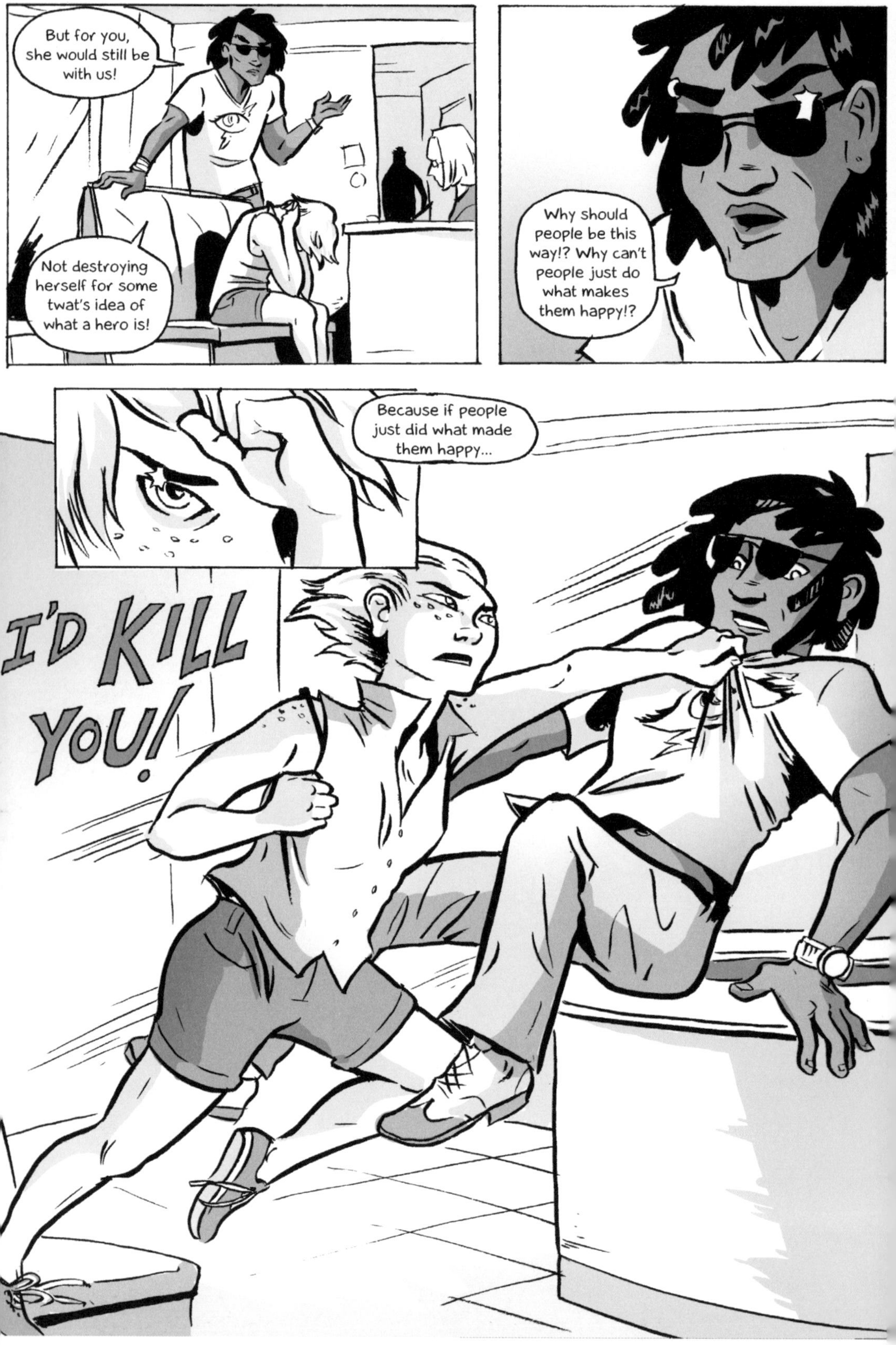
But for you, she would still be with us!
Not destroying herself for some twat's idea of what a hero is!
Why should people be this way!? Why can't people just do what makes them happy!?
Because if people just did what made them happy...
I'D KILL YOU!

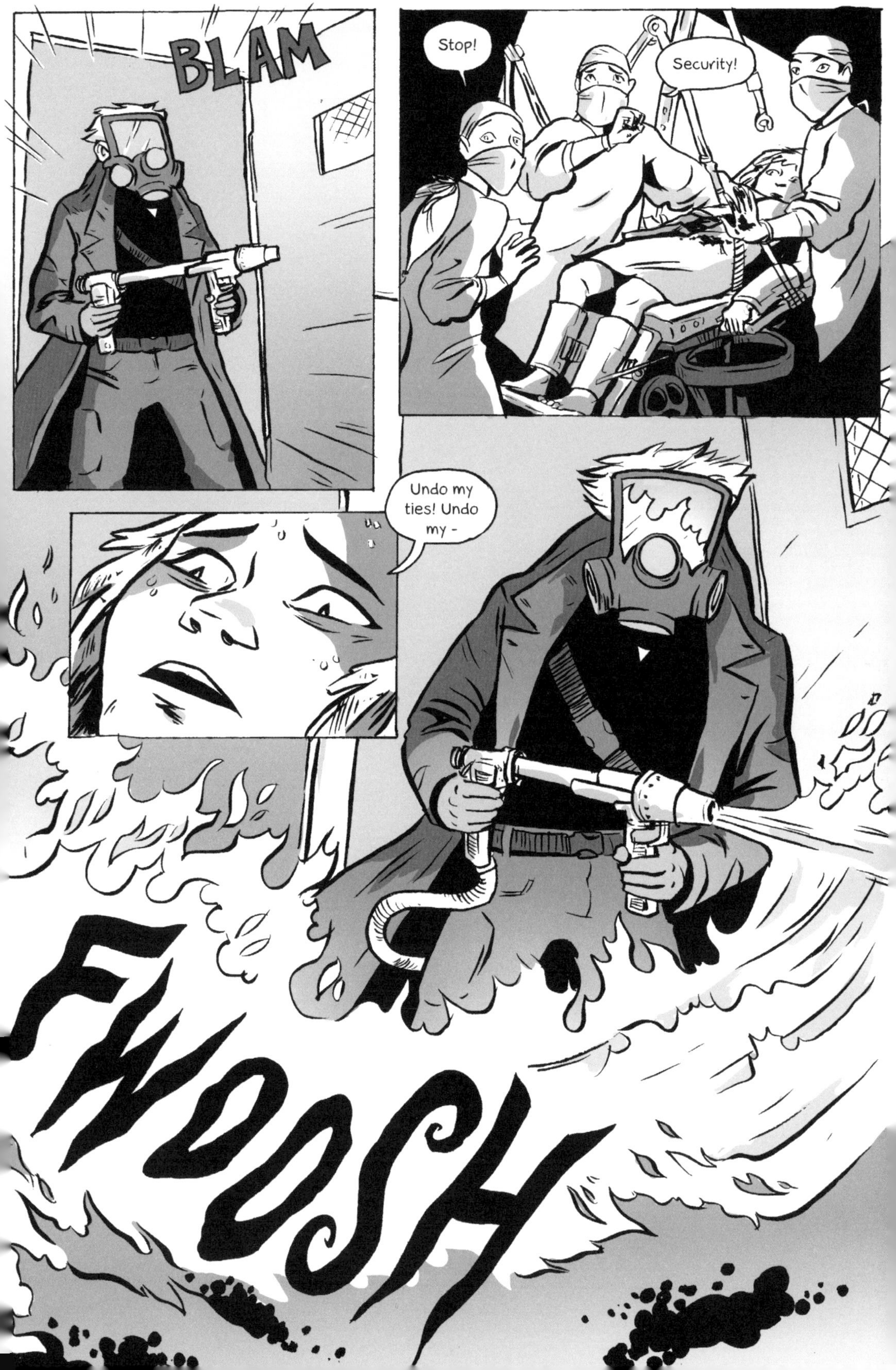
BLAM
Stop!
Security!
Undo my ties! Undo my -
FWOOSH

Back in Islington, Johnny is catching his breath and pouring himself a big glass of Scotch.

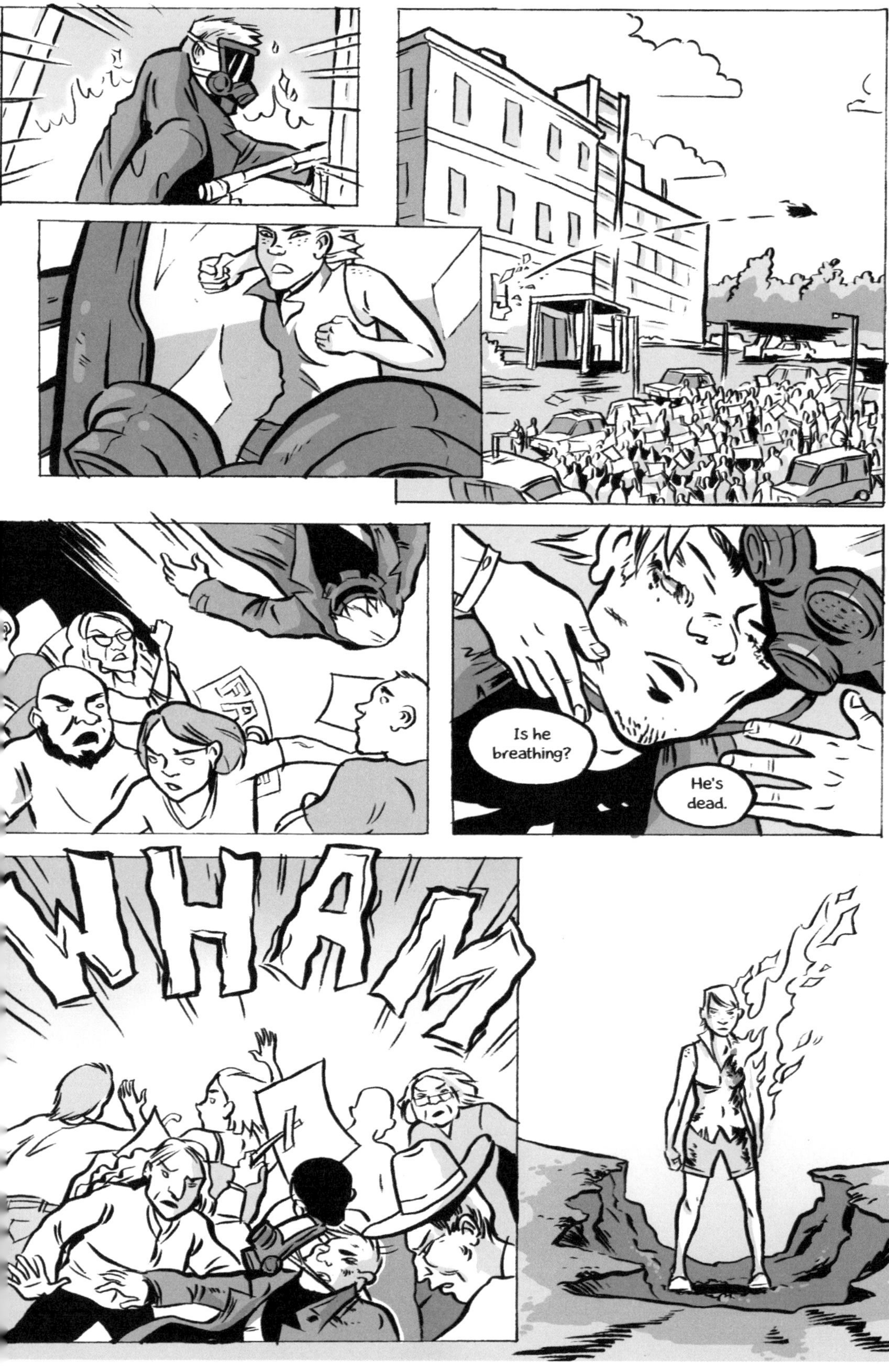
Is he breathing?
He's dead.
WHAM

"My truck!" thought one guy in the back.

Was wondering where you'd scampered off to, Patrick!

Sorry we scared you guys.

Feral...

Don't hurt them. Please.

Don't...

Go home. All of you.

"Boy, seeing that person who I came here to dehumanize stand up for my right to live sure has immediately reversed some of my more hateful beliefs!" - Like, hopefully at least a good bunch of those people?

The US government can afford all kinds of fancy laser restraints, but a TV to watch? Sorry!

You gotta be crazy if you think that the guards at this prison don't make an outrageous salary.

Sometimes I wish people spoke in speech bubbles in real life, so that I could just be all "..."
and everybody would be like, "I see what you're saying".

It wasn't just my stepfather... I killed my mother too. I squashed her like a bug.

You didn't know. She fired a gun at you, you weren't thinking.

I was.

Part of me knew.

Part of me knew she couldn't hurt me.

And I killed her any way.

I'm sorry, is this the part where I cry and promise to only use my powers for good?

Stick to hitting stuff with wrecking balls, Mega Girl, it's what you're good at.

I fantasize about killing people all the time.

... What?

wanted the Prison DJ to do a needle skip in the background, but Molly refused to draw it because it's "insane" and "a bad idea".

"Hi, I'm looking to buy a Mason jar that could fit millions of people? ...Yes, I'll hold."

"You and I are not so very different, Mr. Bond." "Yeah, I know." "...Wait, really?"
"Yeah, we're very similar. Do you want to talk about it?" "I..."

Because I know what it's like to feel alone.

I know what it's like to live in a paper world, to be good at hurting people, to think everybody should just shut up and do what you say.

And then I remember that deep down, people are good, everybody's trying, and nobody deserves respect just for being powerful.

So if I've got the voice in my head that tells me to crush people, then I think you probably have the voice that says the other thing too.

If people keep calling us heroes and villains, they'll never know how close we came to listening to the other voice all those times.

Right now, the best person I know is killing herself to make the world a better place.

The only way I can get her to stop is by making it impossible for things to get any better.

Everything perfect for everyone forever. That's the goal.

That's insane.

Well, it's an insane world. Any other plan couldn't work.

Shoot for the Moon! Then shoot for each of the stars! Then the Sun! 100% Accuracy!

Cleaver, there are real problems out there for us to solve.

I don't know where they all are, I don't know what they all look like, but I'm coming for them, and they should be afraid of me.

You've done some really violent, tragic things. I don't have the authority to forgive you for all of them.

But I can forgive the things you've done to me.

So I forgive you.

And I'm sorry.

And you deserved a better chance than you got. And I wish you weren't sick, and that you didn't hurt so bad.

And I want you to know that even if you hate me, there's at least one other person who knows what it's like, even just a little bit.

I might come back here once in a while and talk with you. Would that be okay?

...Sure.

Good.

The closest you can get to holding his hand.

Mega Girl!

If people were as good as you say they are, they'd know it's your choice to help them.

If your parents hadn't raised you to be a good little girl, they'd be fucked.

The only reason their world makes sense is because you keep it that way.

Do you really think they deserve all of this?

No.

They deserve better.

Superhero

CHAPTER 4

BUSTER THE SUPERDOG

Now you can read along with Alison!
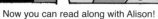

Without an educated population, it doesn't matter what other problems you try to tackle, it's not gonna work.

Think of how much less powerful campaign contributions would be if people had the critical thinking skills to see through advertising?

Think of how many of our problems are based just on pure ignorance, whether it's antiscience people or bigots or whatever. You know?

Is this helpful to you?

Extremely helpful! This is exactly what I wanted to hear.

Okay.

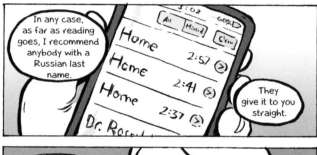

In any case, as far as reading goes, I recommend anybody with a Russian last name.

3:02

All   Missed   60%

Home   2:57

Home   2:41

Home   2:37

Dr. Rosen...

They give it to you straight.

So sorry, I hate to interrupt the conversation, but I just got a bunch of missed calls from home.

Of course. Is everything okay?

I think so, I...

Oh, hey Mom...

Uh huh...

Time to go!

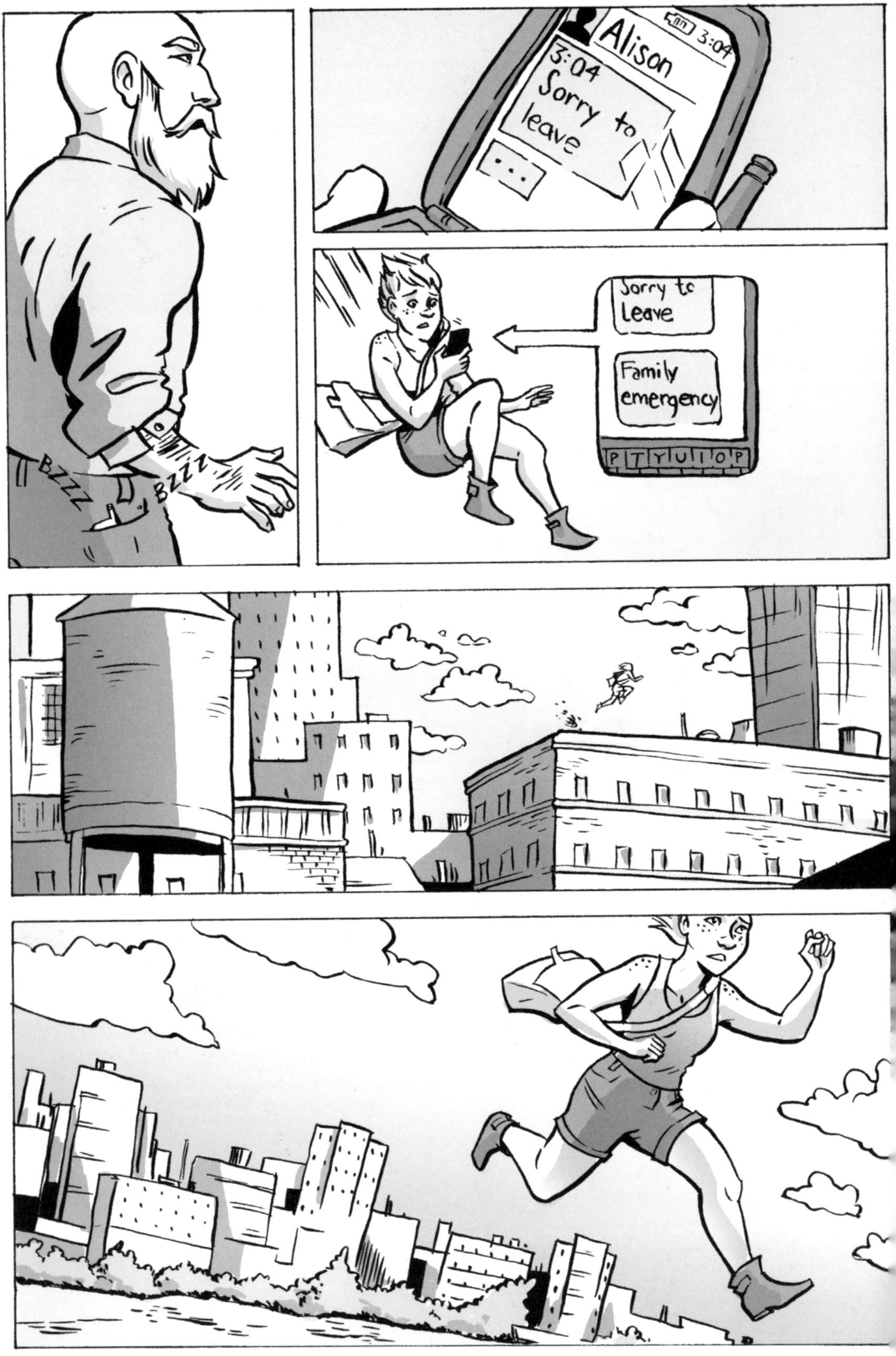
BZZZ
BZZZ
Alison
3:04
3:04
Sorry to leave
...
Sorry to Leave
Family emergency
P T Y U I O P

1991, Westchester, New York

KRAK BOOM

...over in the corner, but let's get you out of the rain!

You can take your pick, but they're all healthy, they've all had their shots.

Thanks so much, Alan, you're a real gem for letting us come out in this nonsense.

No trouble at all. It never really gets that heavy, ya know? It just won't let up is all.

I just hope it's not some kind of Soviet thing gone bad, you know?

If it was an attack, somebody would have taken credit by now. This is just a storm.

You look like a friendly fella!

Don't know if I'd call it "just a storm" when it's covering pretty much the whole Earth.

No, you're right, it's alarming.

I just don't think it's a "Soviet" attack, unless they had a weather machine designed to cover the globe in light thunderstorms. The odds that it's caused by us damaging the Ozone layer seem far more...

Sweetie, what about this little guy?

Possible post-Soviet, fallen-Iron-Curtain weather attacks are important, but just not when there's a pile of puppies in the room.

No, the dog does not also have super strength.

... being a big sister is a lot of responsibility. It's going to be a while before Jennifer can walk and talk and play, and it's all of our job to take care of her.

She's very little, and everything is going to be new to her.

So we get to help her figure everything out. Isn't that neat?

. . .

NO!

The author of this comic wore a fuzzy Dracula cape for most of his childhood. The artist preferred a one-piece Simba suit.

The beard works much better with the moustache, Geoff.

No! Because ... because she's just a BABY, and if she is too small, she can't do anything AT ALL!

I understand, kiddo. Believe it or not, you were small once too. Me and Buster both can remember.

Everybody is little for a little bit. And if we get frustrated and mad at them, it doesn't make them grow up any faster.

But we can love them, and help take care of them, and before long they'll be big kids too!

Right now, everything is new and exciting and a little bit scary for Jennifer. She's just a baby. I think she would probably be really happy to know she had such a great older sister looking after her. Don't you think?

...Yes.

I will use fairy dust to make her grow up, and then I will teach her all the games!

You know, something else, hun...

If you ever want to dress up like a soldier, or a knight, or a cowboy, that's totally okay, and we have those costumes too, so you only have to dress up like a fairy if that's what **you** want to do.

Okay goodbye Daddy I'm a fairy!

An adult human being is the most fearsome, terrifying and powerful animal on the planet, and parenting is the act of creating an adult human being.

No monster in their right mind is about to fuck with that poofy star wand.

We get it Brad, you're in great shape, you can put your shirt backOHMYGOD IT'S MEGAGIRL SOMEBODY INSTAGRAM THIS!!!

"What's wrong with that man?"

"Well, sweetie, it's not that there's anything wrong with him, but he's a homeless man, so he sleeps here in the park sometimes."

"Does he have a house?"

"No, dear, he doesn't."

"But where's his family?"

"I'm afraid I don't know, Alison."

"It's possible that he doesn't have any."

"But... But is he going to be alright?"

Very few Bodhi trees in Westchester, I'm afraid.

Well that's what Daddy's finding out. Your Dad's job is to take care of people who are having a hard time. He makes sure they have what they need, and tries to find them homes and jobs.

Hey Kiddo, what's up? I'm just talking to Chuck here for a minute, everything's fine.

I'm sorry I threw this and it almost hit you. You can have it, if you want.

That's a good frisbee, kid, you should keep it.

Okay. Is there anything I can help?

... What's the dog's name?

His name is Buster.

Hey kiddo, guess what?

Good boy, Buster. That's a good boy.

I'm very proud of you.

That is a cute damn hat on that baby.

Mrs. Green
November 10, 2000

Now I have to say, class, I definitely think we could have put a lot more effort into the test.

Questions one through four were basic, multiple choice questions about the book...

Name: Alison Green
Class: Mrs. Green
Grade: 5
A+ 100/100 + 10 pts extra credit
1. Why is Great job sweetheart!
A. She has a l...

And most of us failed to answer them correctly.

Welcome to your awkward phase, Alison! It all starts with a bad haircut...

For example, who here can tell me why, in the book, Alice begins crying?

Anybody?

I'm sure somebody can tell me the reason that Alice starts crying in the book.

Nobody?

Very well.

A literary critic would tell you that the reference to Alice in Wonderland on this page and Susan Green's subsequent question is apropos given that Alice cries not when she shrinks smaller, but when she grows larger, hearkening back to the major themes of power and isolation found in SFP and indeed in all superhero literature. I as the author can tell you, however, that Alice in Wonderland was just the first book I saw on my bookshelf when I was writing this page. #ThereIsLessGoingOnThanMeetsTheEye

When people give me a teaspoon to scoop sugar for tea I'm like, "We don't have that kind of time!" and go straight for the soup ladle

The only good dad is a weird dad.

Oh, cool!

Are you reading that for the first time?

THE TWO TOWERS

·104· THE TWO TOWERS

asked Merry after a while "I didn't know how you feel with small ragtag dangling...

THE TWO TOWERS

Gandalf laughed ...hobbit! All Wizard ...in their care ...the word, and ...your p...

What?

Is that the first time that you're reading that?

I just... I just like it is all.

No... Me too. I read them all in Grade School.

Oh, you're probably thinking of The Hobbit.

No, I'm not!

There's no way you read all these in grade school.

Yes, there is!

HEY NERD BOY! I KNOW YOU THINK YOU'RE SOMEHOW BEING MADE FUN OF, BUT THAT GIRL IS GENUINELY REACHING OUT TO YOU! YOU KNOW ABOUT FRIENDS, RIGHT? INSTEAD OF CONDESCENDING TO HER IN A PREEMPTIVE SHIELDING OF YOUR BRUISED AND BATTERED EGO, MAYBE JUST TALK TO HER ABOUT THE BOOK YOU BOTH LIKE? DO THIS NOW BEFORE IT'S TOO LATE AND YOU'RE WRITING A COMIC TO DEAL WITH ALL THESE FEELINGS YEARS LATER!

Hey, you're Alison, right?

Uh, yeah?

We're trying to get all the coolest girls in school together so we can claim the table next to the ice cream line. You have a pool at your house, right?

...Yeah!

Cool! You should come sit with us...

Unless you're already sitting down here.

Nope!

Do you know that boy?

Him? No, he's just some... He just started talking to me about his book, and I was like... Uh, who are you, exactly?

Ew, he sits next to me in home room, he's a dork.

You play Neopets, right?

Yes!

Awesome, we all do! Are you signed up for after-school soccer?

No, but I really want to!

Pool=Cool

Buster's just happy to be around all those people.

That footage of those boys walking out of that refinery explosion in Texas? Horrifying. How do you explain that?

I mean everything's just gone upside down. You read about that little girl who went missing in Florida last week? They found her in Alaska, no idea how she got there.

They didn't even look afraid, and the police can't find them now!

It doesn't take a rocket scientist to put it together.

I don't think terrorists would abscond with a young girl and safely deposit her in Alaska just to keep us guessing, Chris.

Oh yeah? Then how do you explain all the crazy stuff in the news? Those mangled up police cars, or that diner where all the silverware just started floating in mid-air?

You have a global network like Al-Qaeda, with limitless resources at their disposal from countries like Iran and North Korea, you think they're gonna try box-cutters again?

We're seeing a massive terror campaign, psychological, chemical, biological...

I'm not a scientist, but I think as long as we keep taking liberties with our planet, we're going to continue to see more and more disturbing phenomena like this.

Spontaneous combustion, explosions, localized magnetic events, I mean, what's it gonna take for us to realize the effect we're having on the Earth and take serious action to stop it?

You think **Global Warming** is responsible for those chopped up cruisers?

That's ridiculous.

ROFF ROFF

What's that, Buster? Fire at the Old Mill?!

Soccer is NOT a team sport.

I have never, ever heard you speak to anyone this way before, and I don't like it one bit.

What has gotten into you? The way you're behaving is atrocious, you're acting like a big bully!

Mom, I'm not being a bully! It's not fair!

I come to all the practices, I work extra hard, I actually watch the videos that coach asks us to watch! And it's like...

Just... Just cut me some slack, okay!?

I get better grades than anyone, I'm the best player on the team, and I just want people to try as hard as I'm trying!

They are trying!

No, they're not! If they were actually trying, they'd be doing as good as me, and they're not!

Sweetheart... Do you think everyone can do what you can do?

Because they can't. You know that, right?

You are very smart, you have a lot of talents and skills that other people don't have.

If you expect everybody to do the things that you can do, you're going to lead a very lonely life.

Susan Green will NOT wait until after the game is done to drop some truth-bombs.

I get it, Katie. Not even Gatorade and orange slices can wipe away the sting of humiliation.

Alison tried to use the Power of Friendship to win the game, but it didn't work.

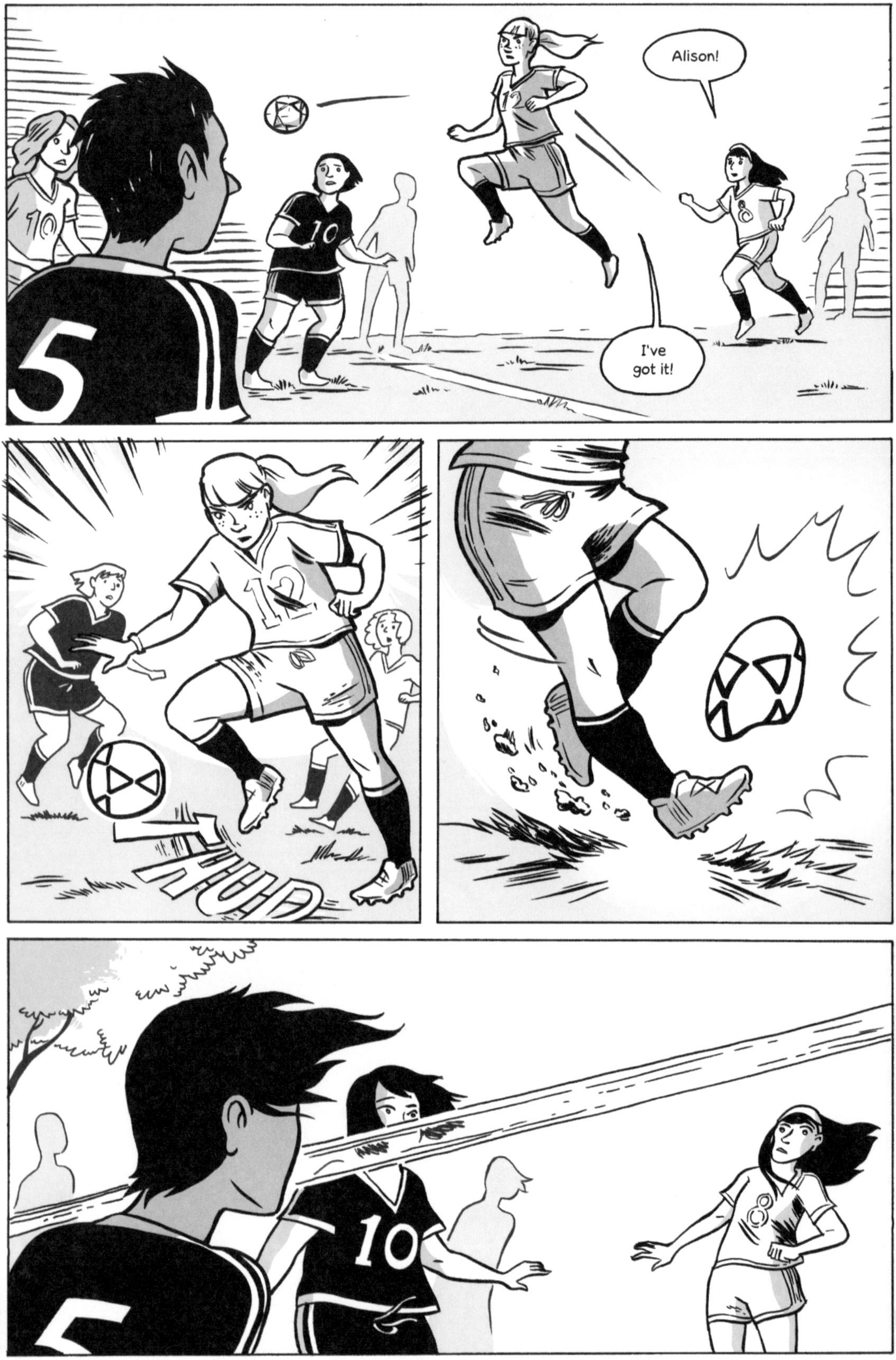
Alison!
I've got it!
THUD

GOOOOOAAAAALLLLL!!!

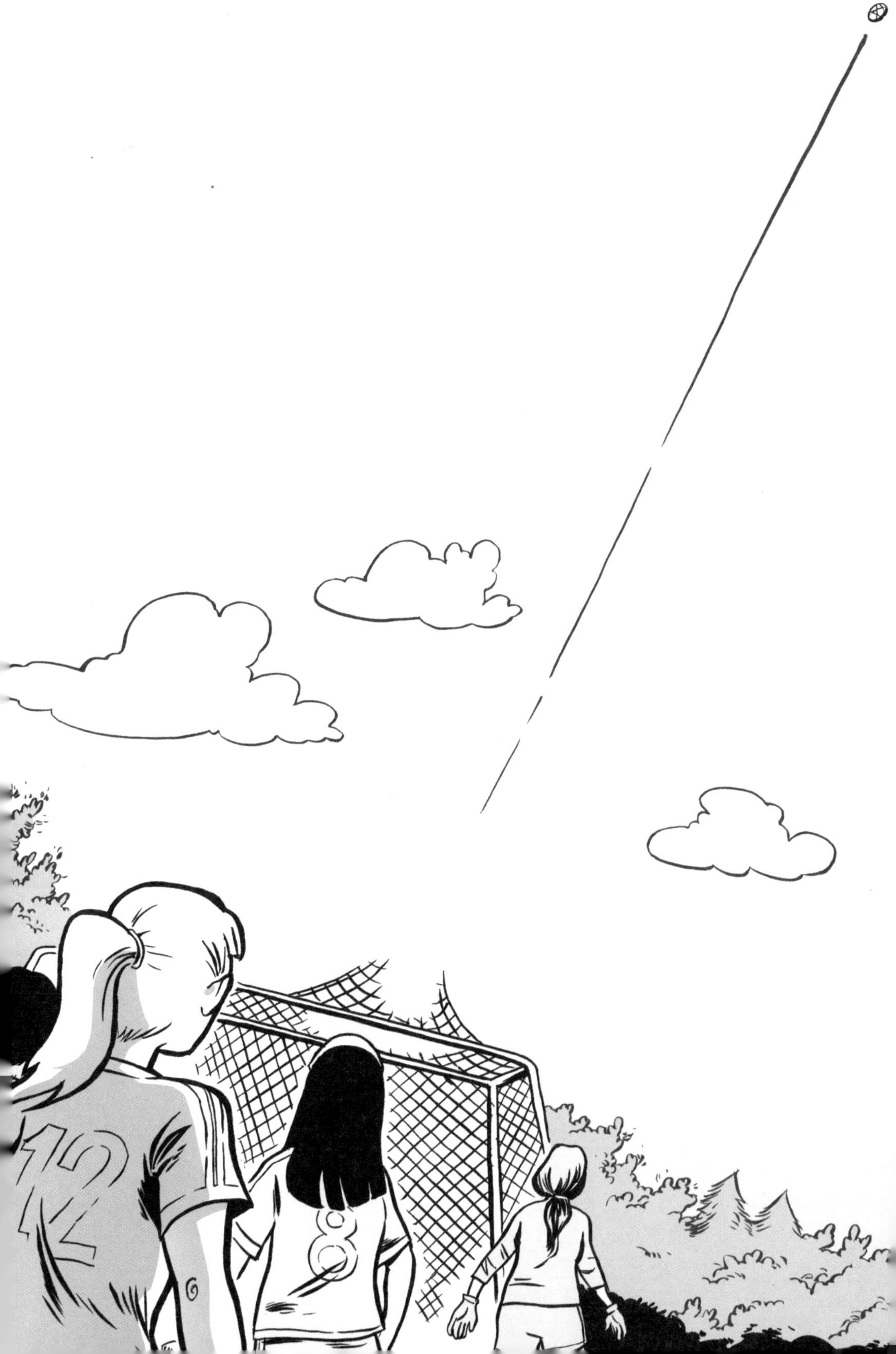

Alison's phone battery doesn't get her invincibility - now that would be a REAL superpower.

No.

You sure kiddo?

It's been two weeks.

I know, I'm still feeling really sick.

Okay, sweetie.

She's got to go back to school sooner or later.

I think she's just nervous about talking to her friends after... you know...

I know... But putting it off for longer will only make it worse.

Do you think we should take her to a doctor?

... For what?

BREAKING: EMERGENCY PRESIDENTIAL ADDRESS

Mom! Dad! Get in here!

That very particular form of guilt that comes from lying to your parents, knowing they know, and knowing they're not going to call you out on it.

Yes, we could have made GW goofy, but I think (hope) he would have gotten it together for a speech about the DISCOVERY OF SUPERHEROES

The Menace show is no one's favorite show.

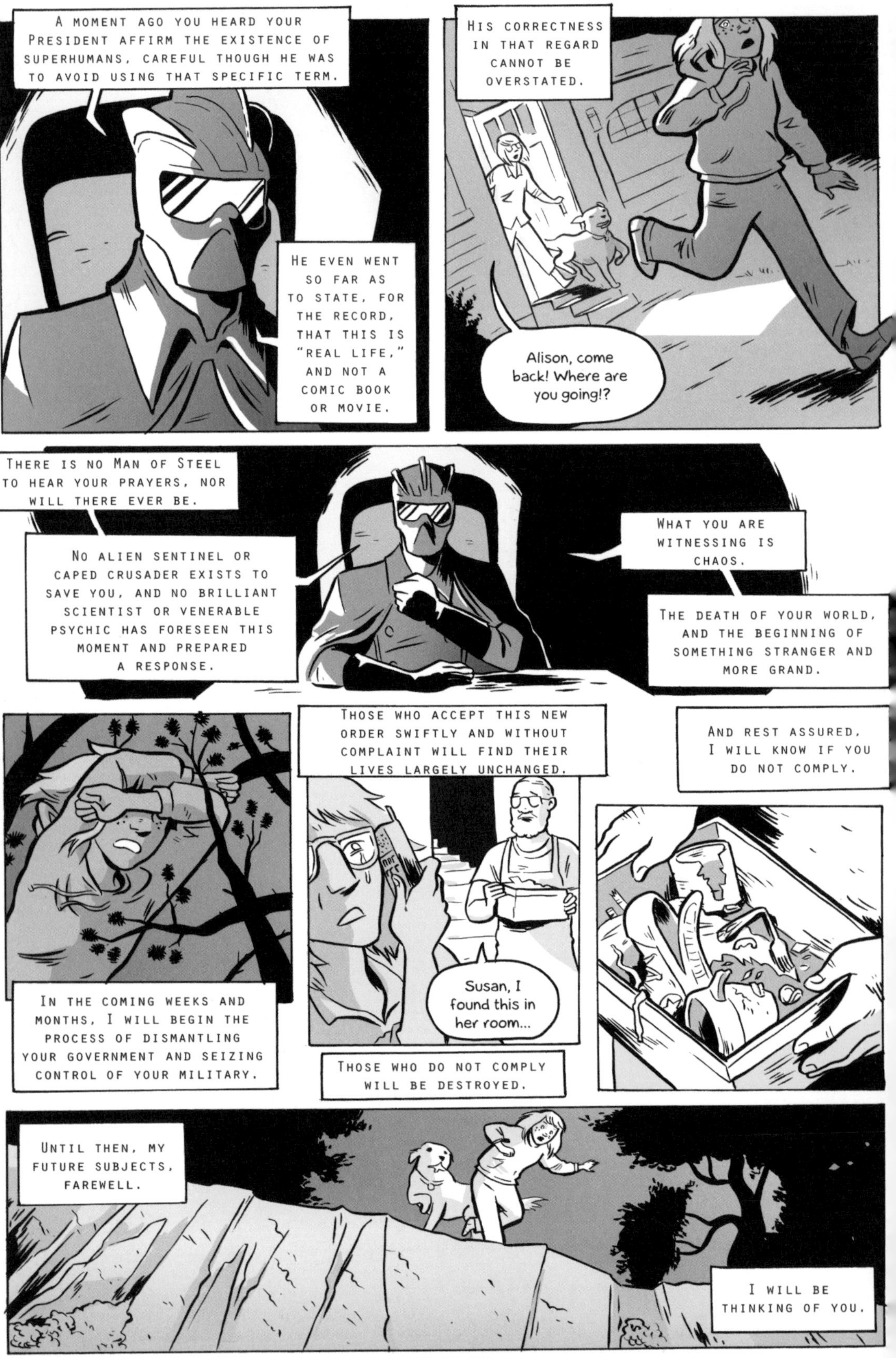
A moment ago you heard your President affirm the existence of superhumans, careful though he was to avoid using that specific term.
He even went so far as to state, for the record, that this is "real life," and not a comic book or movie.
His correctness in that regard cannot be overstated.
Alison, come back! Where are you going!?
There is no Man of Steel to hear your prayers, nor will there ever be.
No alien sentinel or caped crusader exists to save you, and no brilliant scientist or venerable psychic has foreseen this moment and prepared a response.
What you are witnessing is chaos.
The death of your world, and the beginning of something stranger and more grand.
In the coming weeks and months, I will begin the process of dismantling your government and seizing control of your military.
Those who accept this new order swiftly and without complaint will find their lives largely unchanged.
Susan, I found this in her room...
Those who do not comply will be destroyed.
And rest assured, I will know if you do not comply.
Until then, my future subjects, farewell.
I will be thinking of you.

No matter how scary it is to be fourteen and have your whole world change in crazy ways, being able to crush rocks is still really really cool!

AHA HA HA HA HA HA HA HA HA HA HA HA HA HA HA HA

HA HA

heh...

Time to fly.

Sure, my whole life is in shambles and everything I ever knew was a lie, but WEEEEE SUPERPOWERS!!!

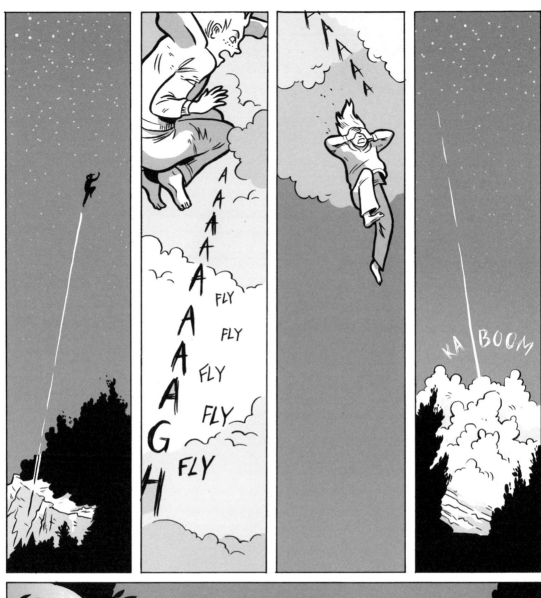

Don't be greedy, it wouldn't really be fair if you had invulnurability, super-strength, AND flight.
No one would want to read that story. Right?

Am I still me?

Aw, Buster.

I love you too...

Good dog.

A cornucopia of emotions

Dude at the bottom of the page is going "Colonel, please read my poems. They're about you, and the mission depends on them." Colonel is like "I don't know how you got that uniform, but you need to put it back where you found it."

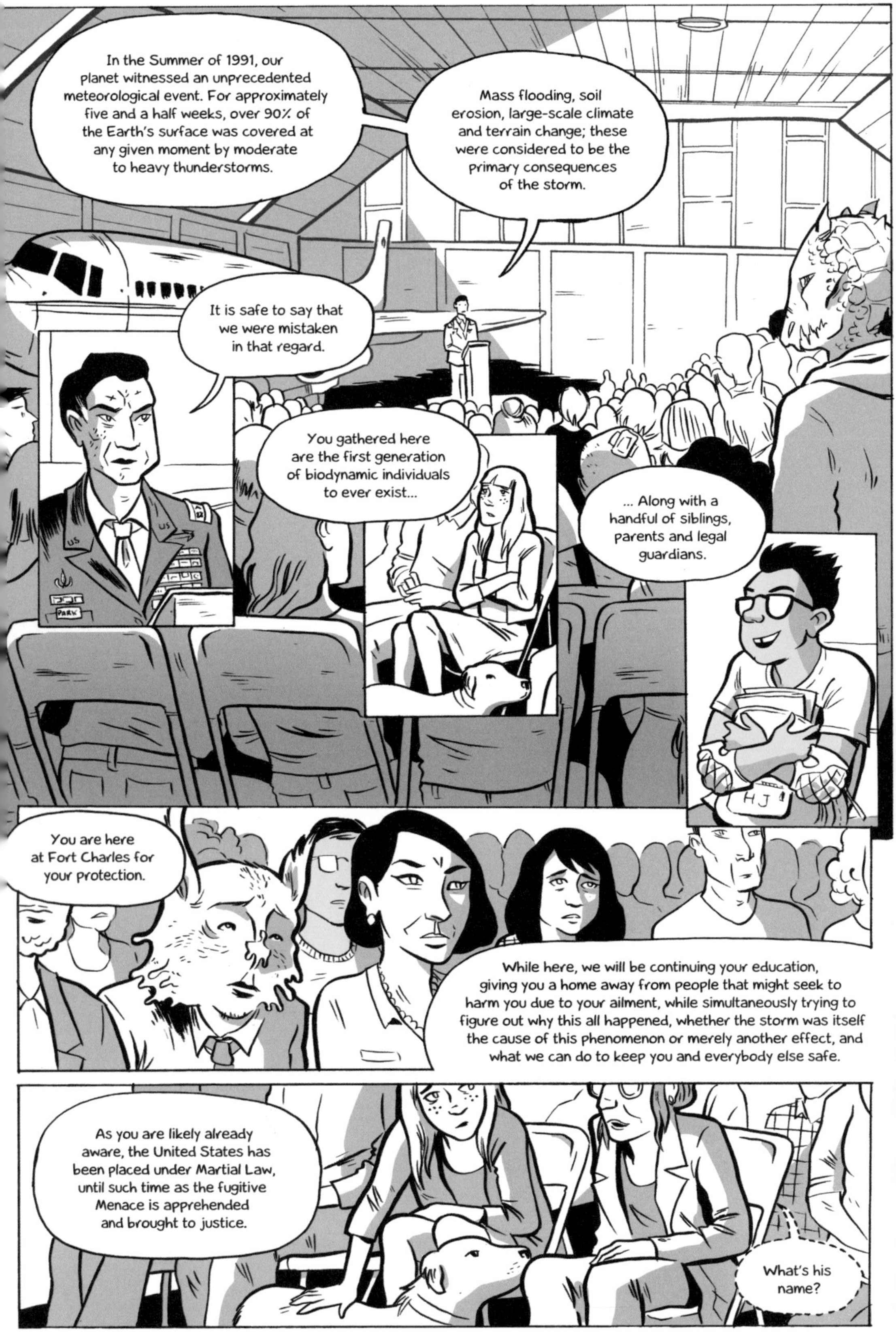
In the Summer of 1991, our planet witnessed an unprecedented meteorological event. For approximately five and a half weeks, over 90% of the Earth's surface was covered at any given moment by moderate to heavy thunderstorms.
Mass flooding, soil erosion, large-scale climate and terrain change; these were considered to be the primary consequences of the storm.
It is safe to say that we were mistaken in that regard.
US
US
PARK
You gathered here are the first generation of biodynamic individuals to ever exist...
... Along with a handful of siblings, parents and legal guardians.
HJ
You are here at Fort Charles for your protection.
While here, we will be continuing your education, giving you a home away from people that might seek to harm you due to your ailment, while simultaneously trying to figure out why this all happened, whether the storm was itself the cause of this phenomenon or merely another effect, and what we can do to keep you and everybody else safe.
As you are likely already aware, the United States has been placed under Martial Law, until such time as the fugitive Menace is apprehended and brought to justice.
What's his name?

You don't *need* camo to cut pies, but it helps more than you'd think!

Wearing elbowpads and kneepads just in case a supervillain attacks explains pretty
much everything you need to know about Pintsize.

I bet the people that are getting killed by those Templar Drones wouldn't mind if a bunch of superheroes flew in and saved the day.

I bet they'd be really grateful, actually.

I need to go. I need to find my parents.

Look, do you really think the government would have made all these bio camps if they didn't kinda want us to figure this out?

They have to say they don't want our help because we're kids and that's the kind of things grown ups have to say.

But I think they really need us.

Look, that's... fine! But there's not, like, a manual on how to be a superhero!

Uh, **wrong!**

It's a shame that you aren't nerdier, otherwise you'd know **exactly** what to do.

SUPERMAN

Here's the manual.

Molly has only read one Superman comic and so that's the one she drew, points to whoever recognizes the cover!

People either read comics or Cosmo, it's true.

Help me think of a better idea than "Mega Girl".

Home again, home again, jiggity ... Oh.

... And we found it early, which almost never happens with this type of cancer, so that's another thing we've got going for us.

Have you gotten a second opinion?

Yuh-huh, this is the second doctor we've spoken to. We didn't wanna tell you or your sister until we were certain.

Now sweetie, I know this is hard to hear, but you've got to know that pancreatic cancer has an extremely poor prognosis generally.

It's got a pretty high fatality rate, relative to other cancers.

We caught it early, and otherwise I'm in good shape. But the five-year-survival for people with my diagnosis is only 20%.

The hard truth is that I'm probably not gonna be around for a whole lot longer.

In case you were wondering, it's super impressive that Alison isn't splintering the table into grief toothpicks right about now.

Pintsize, you should probably really get on that!

I think it's fascinating that so many fictional heroes are orphans. I know it has deep, profound mythological roots that are significant on a Jungian level, but sometimes the choice to make a character an orphan is because the writer is uninterested in dealing with the main character's family, or finds family life an impediment to their main character's identity. Not exactly intellectual laziness, but also not a purely aesthetic choice.

I don't care if you've stared down a Tier One supervillain, nothing is as scary as seeing one of your parents bust out crying.

Invulnurable Schminvulnurable, no one wants to see their kid getting shot.

BUSTER

Hey, Jen. Mind if I come sit?

... Sure.

I still can't believe he's dead. I miss him so much.

He lived until he was 20, that's like a million in dog years.

I know. I just mean... we only buried him a few weeks ago.

It hasn't really hit me yet, it was right before the semester started and I've sort of been diving into this project...

Aren't you cold out here, by the way? It's freezing.

How can you tell?

What do you mean, how can I tell? It's cold.

crushes scouter in hand HER ANGST LEVELS ARE OVER 9000!!!!

We've seen this before in Chapter 2!

C'mooon, that's crazy. You're being soooo overdramatic.

Jen, you don't know what you're talking about. The people who wear shirts like that are very dangerous, it's a federally recognized hate group. Are you hanging out with people that wear those shirts, or have tattoos with a skeleton with a cape on it?

No, YOU don't know what you're talking about! Not **everybody** who wears these attacks superheroes, okay? That's like ... a handful of people.

They don't attack superheroes, Jen. They attack biodynamic people, usually in the third tier, usually without an anomaly that allows them to defend themselves. Is that a group you want to be a part of?

I don't want to be a part of anything! I don't want to be a part of this... this family, or this world, or anything! It all sucks, and I just can't take it anymore!

You have no idea what it's like, okay? No idea! There's a whole world full of people like me, that are fucking... **BYSTANDERS**! That's what you call us, right? **BYSTANDERS**!? What is there that I can possibly do that's gonna matter to anybody?

Forget about the fact that I'm the little sister of fucking **MEGA GIRL**, and Mom and Dad are constantly checking CNN to see if you've demolished a new building, or that I had to change schools because you pulled your mask off. **My life doesn't matter.** Do you know what that feels like!?

First of all, I know literally nobody that refers to chromosomally stable people as "bystanders."

First things first

Guidance counselors in the world of SFP have their work CUT OUT FOR THEM!

Of course you made a difference. You're fucking Mega Girl.

You're right. There were a couple of times where things were very chaotic, and I punched some robots and then things got better. Hooray for me.

So what, you regret saving the world!?

I regret thinking that was enough.

Look, Jennifer, you can't... If you put all the pressure on us, we're not going to make it.

What!? I'm not putting pressure on you!

You are, though! The people that worship superheroes or the people that hate us, they're both making it about us.

And we're going to let you down, because we don't really know what's going on more than regular people, and we can't really do that much more than regular people.

Yes you can! You're invincible! You've got super-strength! You can do fucking anything!

I can't save Dad.

Will Alison's super-strength be a match for the collosal heaviness of her statement in the last panel?!

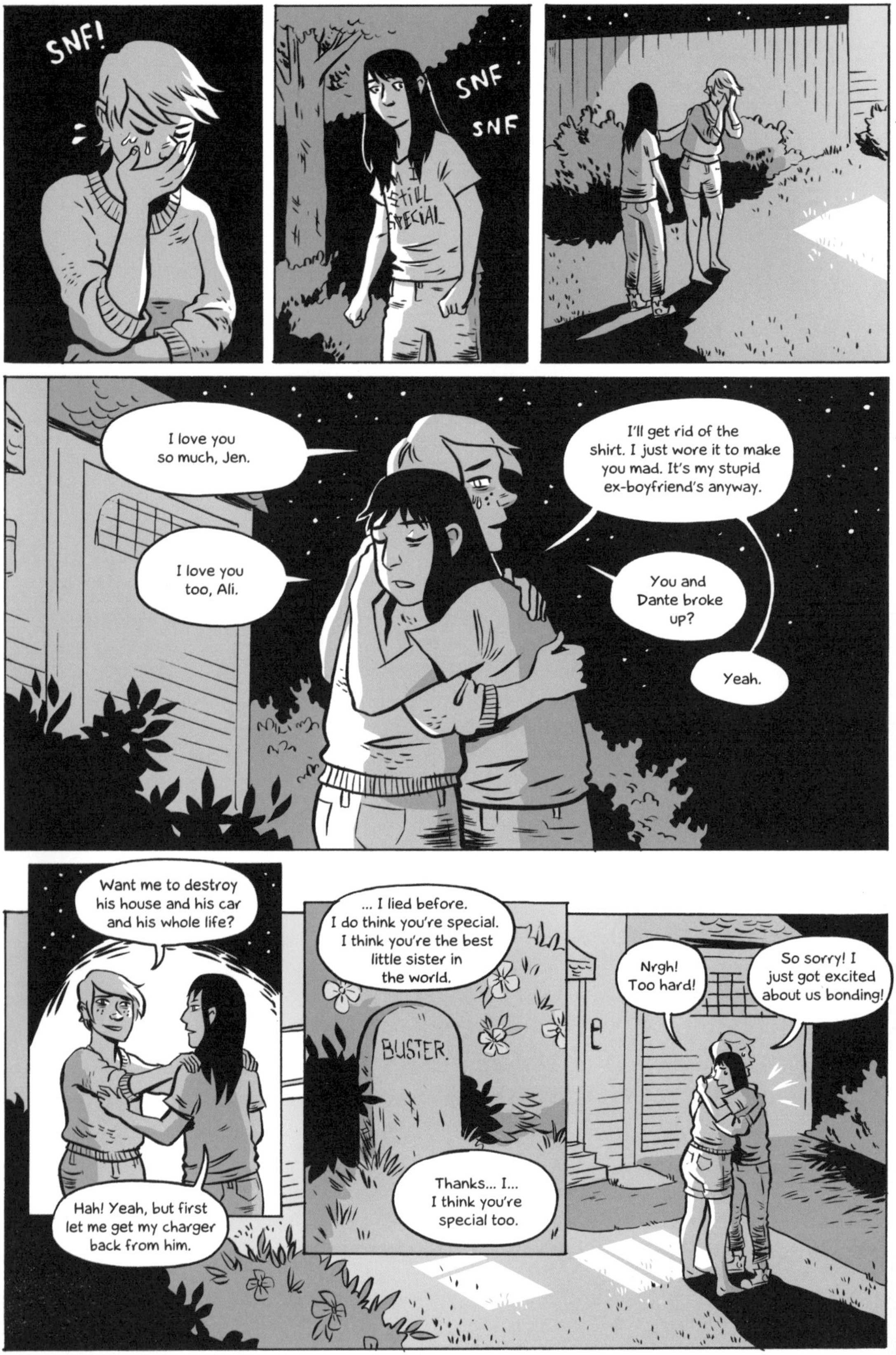
SNF!
SNF
SNF
I'M I STILL SPECIAL
I love you so much, Jen.
I love you too, Ali.
I'll get rid of the shirt. I just wore it to make you mad. It's my stupid ex-boyfriend's anyway.
You and Dante broke up?
Yeah.
Want me to destroy his house and his car and his whole life?
Hah! Yeah, but first let me get my charger back from him.
... I lied before. I do think you're special. I think you're the best little sister in the world.
BUSTER.
Thanks... I... I think you're special too.
Nrgh! Too hard!
So sorry! I just got excited about us bonding!

Thanks for reading!

Alison's story continues at
www.strongfemaleprotagonist.com,
where it updates twice weekly.

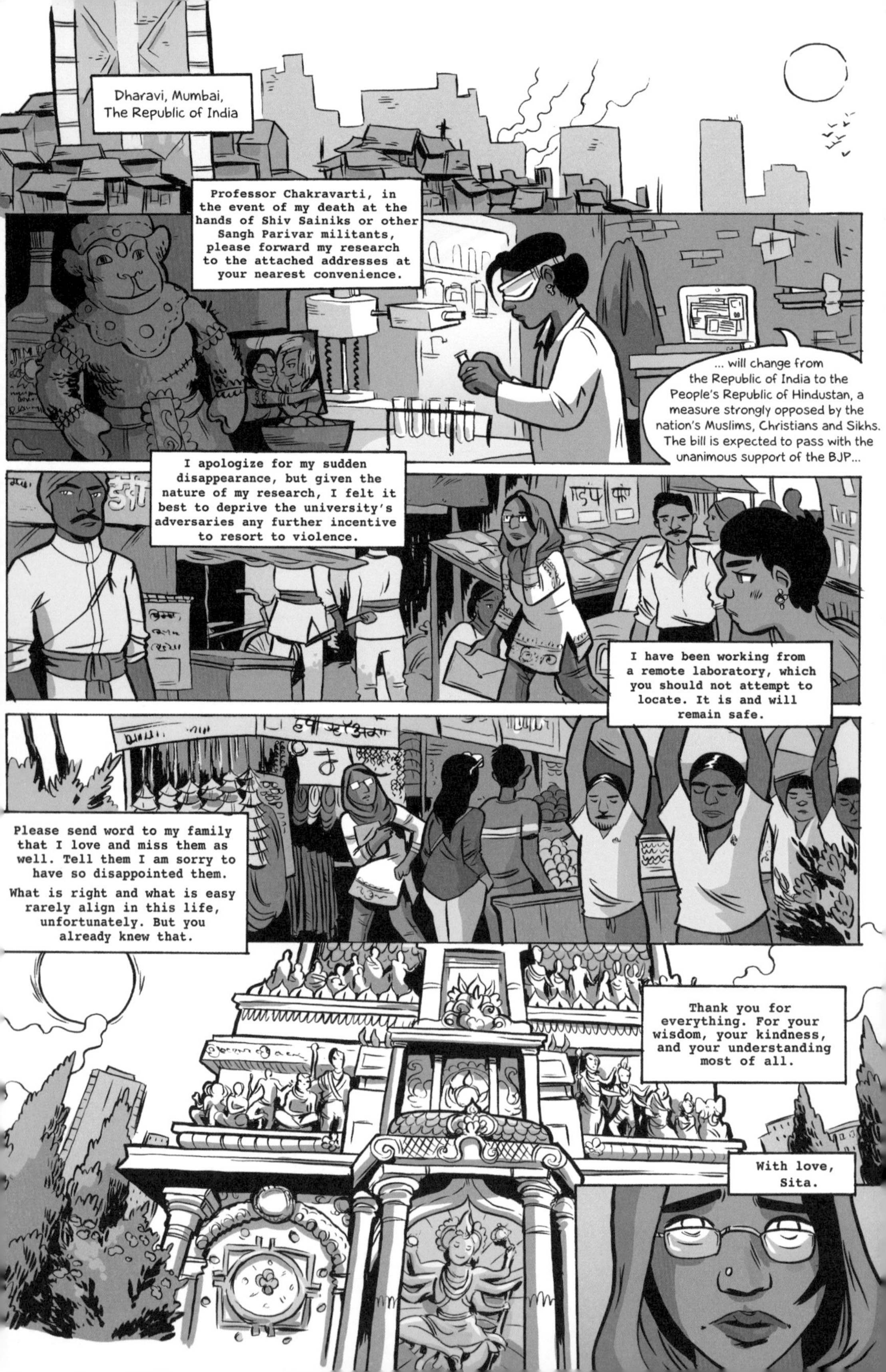

Dharavi, Mumbai, The Republic of India
Professor Chakravarti, in the event of my death at the hands of Shiv Sainiks or other Sangh Parivar militants, please forward my research to the attached addresses at your nearest convenience.
... will change from the Republic of India to the People's Republic of Hindustan, a measure strongly opposed by the nation's Muslims, Christians and Sikhs. The bill is expected to pass with the unanimous support of the BJP...
I apologize for my sudden disappearance, but given the nature of my research, I felt it best to deprive the university's adversaries any further incentive to resort to violence.
I have been working from a remote laboratory, which you should not attempt to locate. It is and will remain safe.
Please send word to my family that I love and miss them as well. Tell them I am sorry to have so disappointed them.
What is right and what is easy rarely align in this life, unfortunately. But you already knew that.
Thank you for everything. For your wisdom, your kindness, and your understanding most of all.
With love, Sita.

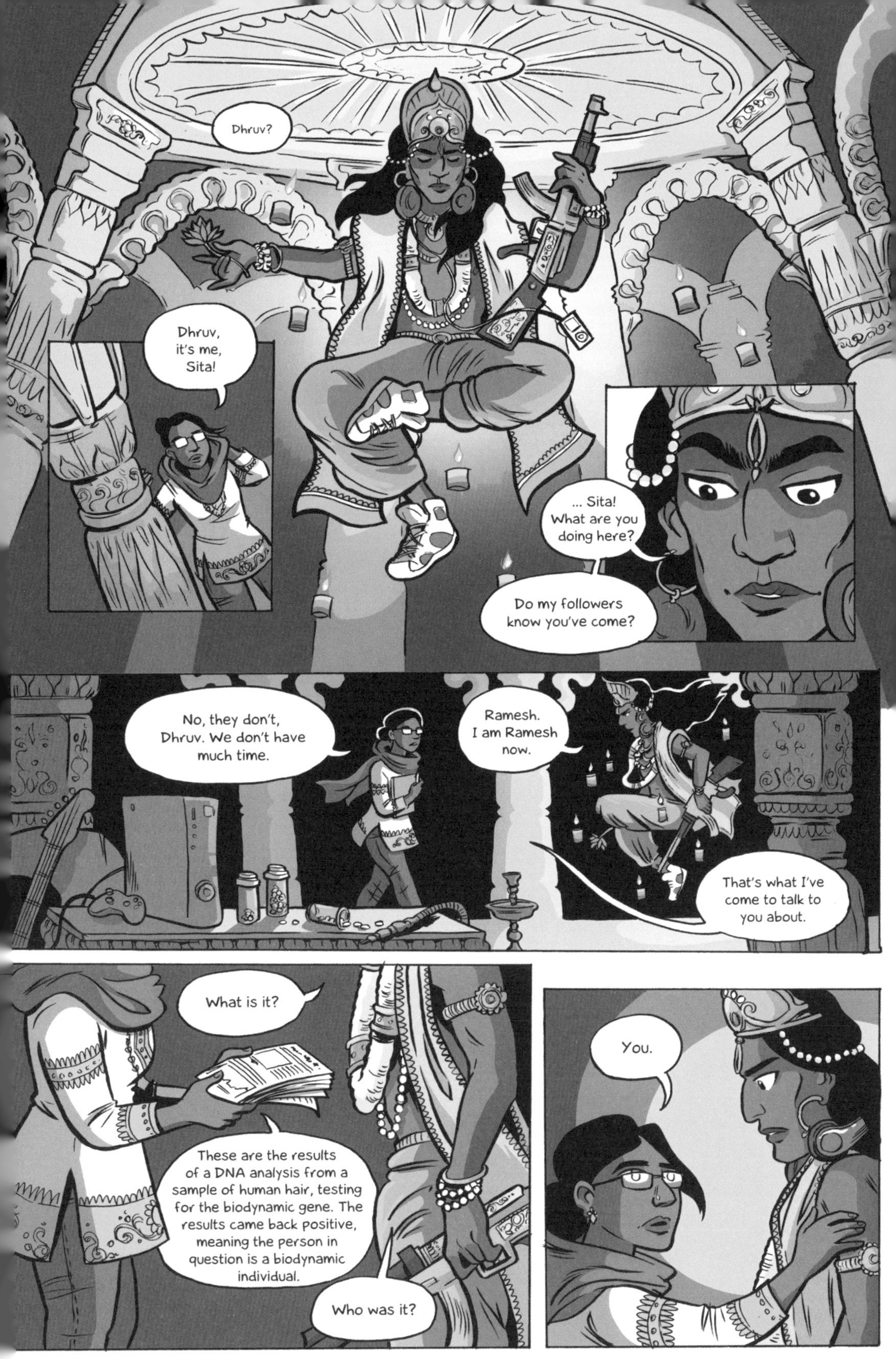
Dhruv?
Dhruv, it's me, Sita!
... Sita! What are you doing here?
Do my followers know you've come?
No, they don't, Dhruv. We don't have much time.
Ramesh. I am Ramesh now.
That's what I've come to talk to you about.
What is it?
These are the results of a DNA analysis from a sample of human hair, testing for the biodynamic gene. The results came back positive, meaning the person in question is a biodynamic individual.
Who was it?
You.

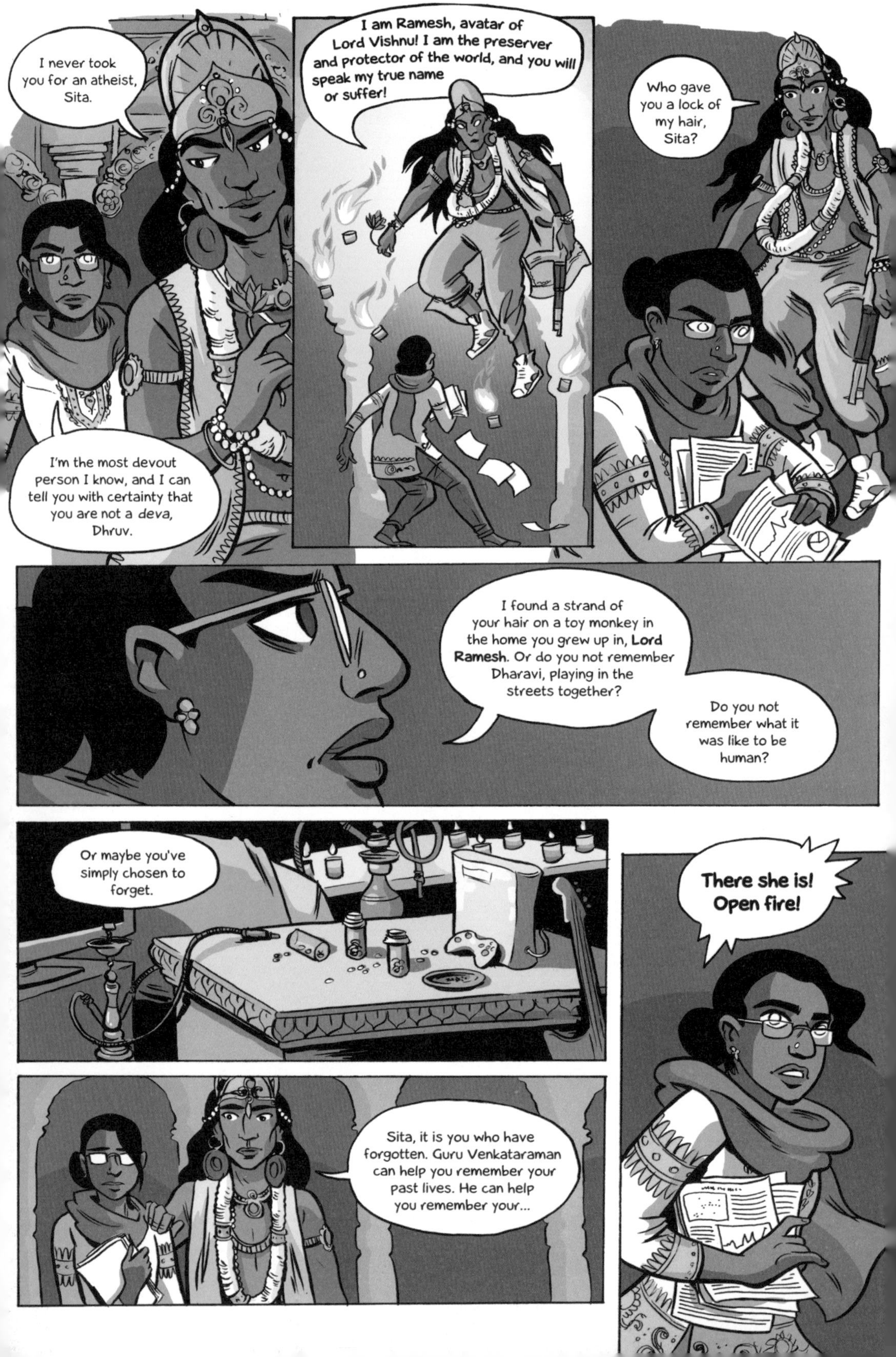
I never took you for an atheist, Sita.
I'm the most devout person I know, and I can tell you with certainty that you are not a *deva*, Dhruv.
I am Ramesh, avatar of Lord Vishnu! I am the preserver and protector of the world, and you will speak my true name or suffer!
Who gave you a lock of my hair, Sita?
I found a strand of your hair on a toy monkey in the home you grew up in, **Lord Ramesh**. Or do you not remember Dharavi, playing in the streets together?
Do you not remember what it was like to be human?
Or maybe you've simply chosen to forget.
Sita, it is you who have forgotten. Guru Venkataraman can help you remember your past lives. He can help you remember your...
There she is! Open fire!

After her! She cannot leave the grounds!

Lord Ramesh, if you would consider destroying the *asura* before she can escape...

She is no asura. She is Lakshmi, my wife. I cannot destroy her.

... What makes you think that, my Lord?

I do not think it, I know it. I am a God, aren't I?

Aren't I?

Of course you are, my Lord. Of course you are.